T0039360

A History of
St Peter's Church,
Brighton

A History of
St Peter's Church,
Brighton

P.D.W. Nicholl

authorHOUSE®

AuthorHouse™ UK Ltd.
1663 Liberty Drive
Bloomington, IN 47403 USA
www.authorhouse.co.uk
Phone: 0800.197.4150

Published by AuthorHouse 12/13/2013

ISBN: 978-1-4918-8741-7 (sc)
ISBN: 978-1-4918-8742-4 (e)

The author would like to record his grateful thanks to all those who have assisted him in producing this book, but especially to Vivien Nicholl for all her support, and to Jan Lank for her help with the proof-reading. Other contributors are mentioned in the notes at the back of the book.

Grateful thanks, also goes to the helpful staff at the places of reference used in researching the book: The East Sussex Record Office in Lewes; the History Room at the Brighton Museum; the Brighton Library; and the Keep, Woollards Way, Brighton

CONTENTS

1. Beginnings

This is the story of a church. In relation to the other great churches that have been built down the centuries throughout the land of Britain, it is a fairly young structure. But it is a church that is deeply loved by the people of Brighton, for along with the Pavilion and the Pier, this grand old building dominates the cityscape. In his book, "Brave New City", Anthony Seldon· describes it as "a building of national importance . . . . one of the finest Gothic Revival churches in Britain, designed in the decorated and perpendicular styles."[2]

From the top of Bear Road or sitting on the Brighton Wheel, St Peter's can be seen nestling in the distance, while a southbound journey down the Ditchling Road or along the London Road draws the majestic view of its stately architecture closer every minute. When you travel past St Peter's you know you are entering into the heart of the city, and as you do so, you cannot fail to admire the magnificence of its beauty and grandeur.

1818 was the year it all started. The population of Brighton had grown rapidly in the fifty years prior to this date. From about 2,000 in 1750 it increased to around 4,000 when the Prince of Wales—later to become Prince Regent and then King George IV—first came to the town in 1783. New streets and houses were then built up and his palace, the Royal Pavilion that brought the town to prominence, itself became the centre piece of all this development in 1787.

Then new areas were developed—Kemp Town to the east and Brunswick to the west—and by 1821, the population had risen to 24,000 inhabitants. However there were only two churches in the town—the parish church of St Nicholas and the Chapel Royal—and this was clearly inadequate to meet the needs of this growing population, especially as the majority of places in church were rented to worshippers.

With the massive population shifts and growth of this time, this must have been a national problem, for in 1818 an Act of Parliament was passed to "build and promote the building of additional churches in populous parishes." This led to a meeting of the Brighton Vestry, attended by church ratepayers, on 5th November 1818, at which a resolution was passed to build another church.[3]

The Act had set up Commissioners for Building New Churches, and they agreed to loan £15,000 for the new church in Brighton. This loan was due to be paid back over five years at £3,000 a year. When it was realised that this amount could not be afforded by church ratepayers, there was a successful renegotiation to extend the period over ten years, which reduced the annual premium to £1,500.

A competition for the design of this new church building was then organised and it was won by Charles Barry (1795-1860). He was a relatively unknown architect at this time, and the design of St Peter's was his first important work. It was to be a big stepping stone for his career as it gave him the necessary prestige to lead on to his other notable achievements. For he was going to be able to go on to design many famous buildings in England including the Houses of Parliament and Highclere Castle (now known to many television viewers as Downton Abbey).

At this time Thomas Read Kemp (1782-1844), who is famous for the development of Kemp Town, was the Lord of the Manor in Brighton. He had studied theology at Cambridge University and was a regular preacher at St James Non-Conformist Chapel in Kemp Town. When the building of St Peter's was mooted he agreed to act as treasurer of the appeal, and his signature is the first on the legal document[4] conveyancing the land that the church was to be built on.

The other signatories on this document included several prominent land owners of the time. They were:

- Charles Scrase Dickens the elder
- Charles Scrase Dickens the younger
- John Wichelo
- Nathaniel Kemp of Ovingdean Hall, the uncle of Thomas Read Kemp
- Philip Mighell
- Thomas Attree, the son of William Attree (known locally as the King of Brighton)
- Robert James Carr, who was the vicar of Brighton from 1804-1824 and Dean of Hereford from 1820

The land chosen for the site of the new church was to the north of the Steine which is the area where the valley, which runs down from Patcham through Preston along the line of the London Road, meets the sea. St Peter's was built on a traffic island between York Place and Richmond Place. Originally the Ditchling Road ran down to the Steine on this site, but the road was ended further north, while the Lewes Road was diverted to the east, when the church was built. Thus the building of the church took 204 yards off the Ditchling Road and 77 yards off the Lewes Road.

The document also states that because of the lay of the land that was acquired for its building, the church was going to have to face north since the allotted land went north/south rather than the traditional east/west. However St Peter's is not alone in Brighton for having been built in the "non-traditional direction" for there are many other churches in the city which have been erected in all sorts of directions. There was also a stipulation that no corpse was to be interred "either within or without the walls," and St Peter's has never had its own graveyard.

In 1824, Dr Robert James Carr was about to be made Bishop of Chichester. On Saturday 8th May that year, he laid the foundation stone of St Peter's Church. The ceremony started with a procession from the Old Ship Hotel to the site of the new Church near the Level.[5] The parade included clergy, school children, magistrates, a band, a choir, and various local dignitaries and officials. They began with the singing of Psalm 100, "All People That On Earth Do Dwell". [6] Charles Barry then presented Dr Carr with a silver trowel to lay the first stone, after depositing coins of the current reign and medals commemorating events of the period. The inscription on the stone read:

"The first stone of this church, intended to be dedicated to Peter, was laid by Robert James Carr D.D., Dean of Hereford and Vicar of Brighton on Saturday 8ᵗʰ May 1824 in the fifth year of the Reign of His Most Sacred Majesty, George the IV, of the United Kingdom of Great Britain and Ireland, King, Defender of the Faith—Charles Barry, architect. William Ranger, builder."

After this the stone was lowered and adjusted, the following prayer was said by the Rev J.H. Taylor, the senior curate of Brighton. It was a splendid prayer for the start of such a venture, including, as it did, requests for blessings for future generations. Thus is worth recording in full, since much of the rest of this book will show how, amidst all the ups and downs of church life, these requests have continued to be granted:

O Almighty God, the Creator and Governor of the Universe whose superintending Provenience surveyeth and directeth all thy works, look down, we humbly beseech thee, with an eye of mercy upon us thy unworthy servants, presuming to approach the throne of thy grace, under a consciousness of our manifold infirmities, with the zealous but imperfect tribute of prayer and praise. Thou, O Lord, hast thine abiding place in that light, to which no man can approach: Thou dwellest not in temples made with hands: Heaven is thy throne, earth is thy footstool; yet hast Thou been pleased in compassion to mankind to adopt the revelations of thy will to their limited understandings; to speak after the manner of men because of the infirmity of our flesh. Thou seekest those to worship thee who worship thee not merely in forms of goodness, but in spirit and in truth:—yet Thou hast deigned in mercy to our weakness to permit and enjoin that we should create altars to Thy name, and dedicate houses of prayer to Thy service, so that we may be led and reminded by the force of precept and example and by the assembling of ourselves together, to offer under Thee the sacrifice of praise and thanksgiving and to render the honour due unto Thy name. Vouchsafe, then, we beseech thee, glorious Lord, to prosper the work we have in hand: May the foundations of the house we would this day establish to Thy glory be surmounted by a godly superstructure, dedicated to Thee, hallowed by Thy favour and fitted for Thy service; and may all those who, in future generations, shall visit this Thy House of Prayer, be made duly sensible by Thy grace of the end of their creation; may they remember that they are not their own, but that they are bought with a price, and may they thus be led to glorify Thee on earth, and to become fellow citizens with thy saints, and of the household of God built upon the foundation of the Apostles and Prophets, an holy temple to the Lord, of which Jesus Christ himself is the chief corner stone. Accept, we beseech thee, O Lord, these prayers of thy unworthy servants: Bless the King and all that are in authority under him, and all orders and degrees of men in Thy holy Church: reclaim those who have wandered from Thy fold: call the heathen to a knowledge of Thy salvation: and dispose all mankind to serve Thee in pureness of living and truth, to Thy honour and glory, who livest and reignest ever, one God world without end—AMEN

This was followed by the singing of the hymn, "O Lord Send out Thy Light and Truth," and the formalities were concluded with the National Anthem. Then there was a procession, led by a marching band, from the site to the Old Ship Hotel where a dinner was to be held that evening.

At the time of the building the committee had placed an advertisement which read as follows: "To the proprietors of stone Quarries. The Committee for superintending the erection of a New Church in the Parish of Brighton will feel obliged to any gentlemen who would do them the favour of sending specimens of the different Free Stone in the county of Sussex, together with the probable price at per foot cube at which it can be delivered to the town of Brighton. It is requested that the specimens do not exceed a foot cube and that they be sent to the offices of Messrs Attree and Cooper, Ship Street, Brighton as soon as convenient."

However the church was eventually built with Portland stone. This was an excellent choice as the magnificence of the building nearly two hundred years later still owes much to the way in which this gleaming white stone catches the sun. The church was designed by Barry in the Perpendicular and Decorated styles of the fourteenth century, and is one of the earliest and finest Gothic revival churches in the country, as well as being the first great nineteenth century Brighton church.

William Ranger's building work took over three years and St Peter's was opened on 24th July 1828 in the presence of Princess Augusta, the sister of King George IV. The local newspaper[7] reported:

CONSECRATION OF THE NEW CHURCH

> Yesterday the New Church of St Peter was consecrated, with the solemnities usual on such occasions, by the Right Rev. the Lord Bishop of Chichester. An impressive sermon was preached by the Rev. H.M. Wagner, the Vicar of this town, from the second book of Chronicles, 7.1, "Now when Solomon had made an end of praying, the fire came down from Heaven, and consumed the burnt offering and the sacrifices, and the glory of the Lord filled the house."

This text comes in the context of the consecration of Solomon's Temple in Jerusalem, and was therefore appropriate for such an occasion. One feature of the opening ceremony was a festival of sacred music in which it was said that some of the most distinguished singers and musical celebrities of the time took part.[8] The Bishop of Chichester then presided over an evening banquet, which included the introduction of a model of the church in biscuit!

Barry's initial intention was that St Peter's should have a spire, and it is said that he expressed regret that this was not built. It is likely that the cost of erecting a spire on top of the tower was prohibitive[9] and, in any case, it is felt that the absence of such a structure has caused no detrimental effect to the overall beauty of the building. In fact, with St Peter's being built in a valley, such a spire would not be seen from much of a distance, unlike Chichester Cathedral whose spire can be viewed for miles around due to the flatness of the surrounding land. Rather than this, the visual effect of St Peter's lies in its domination of the valley through his size and beauty. A contemporary account described the new church as "a parallelogram with a semi-hexagonal termination at the north and a handsome tower at the south."

The tower is certainly a Brighton landmark, for it still performs its original design purpose of providing a grand termination to the north end of the Steine. The original church measured 150 feet by 70 feet and had galleries to the east, south and west. There was an organ behind the south gallery; while at the north (front) end of the church were a pair of pulpits—one for the leader of the service and one for the preacher. To those who find this a bit daunting, it should be remember that the congregation in the galleries were probably on the same level as the occupiers of these pulpits, while Barry's high vaulted ceilings also help us understand the appropriateness of these structures.

Behind them was the semi-hexagonal apse, with its three main windows, that included room for a small vestry. At the front of the church were three wooden panels in dead gold. On each of them were inscribed the Ten Commandments, the Creed and the Lord's Prayer, with the initial letters in red and the other lettering in blue.

The cost of the new church was paid for partly out of the parish poor-rate, and partly from voluntary subscriptions. The architect's original estimate for the cost of the building was £14,703, 3s, 5d while the actual cost was closer to £16,000. According to Henry Wagner (1792-1870), who had succeeded Carr as the vicar of Brighton, a position he held until 1870, the total cost was £21,865, 5s. Dr John Hannah, the second incumbent at St Peter's reckoned that in 1874 it would have cost £35,000. The Trustees from the outset were Thomas Read Kemp, Lord Egremont, the Lord Lieutenant of Sussex, Sir David Scott and Dr Robert James Carr, the Bishop of Chichester, before he was translated to become Bishop of Worcester in 1831.

The church had seats for 1800 people, half of which were free seats.[10] The Commissioners for Building New Churches had demanded, as a condition of their grants and loans, that a large proportion should be free. The figure was initially set at 1,100, reduced by pressure from the parish to 900 free seats. The letting of the rest of the pews helped to repay the debt that had been incurred in the building of the church, for the total cost was estimated at £20,365.

One contemporary description of the new church read as follows:

"Erected at the north end of the town, near the junction of the routes from London and Lewes, in the year 1826, it is a fine and beautiful gothic structure and one of the most pleasing specimens in England within the last twenty years. The expense was about £20,000, for which an edifice of ample dimensions has been constructed, with a sufficient display of solid and well arranged ornaments . . . . The church consists of a lofty nave and two side aisles up wards of one hundred feet in length, the centre projecting in a semi-octagonal sweep, ornamented with three handsome windows, with ramified tracery: there are parapets and good pinnacles and buttresses throughout; the parapet of the centre aisle is waved and pierced with quatrefoils, and the pinnacles at either extremity are larger and loftier than the intermediate ones. At the west end is a neat tower, with deep belfry windows, some fretwork and four tall pinnacles; also four handsome Clock-faces. On three of its sides is a lofty and grand projecting porch or vestibule, of a novel design, with beautiful ogee arches and clustered pillars, and turret-like spiral pinnacles at the angles. The lower part of this tower forms a convenient vestibule or hall, with a coved ceiling, forty feet high, and a double staircase to the galleries. In the interior, the nave is nearly fifty feet high, and the aisles thirty, separated on each side by five arches, resting on lofty and light columns, the centre moulding piercing the capital, and rising to the spring of the roof, which is vaulted throughout in imitation of stone, producing a very happy appearance. The whole is very appropriately fitted up; the pews of the colour of oak, and the fronts of the galleries of stone. At the east end is a neat stone altar screen of fret-work, and at the opposite end a handsome gallery, arched in imitation of stone, above which is a second of oak, containing the organ, an instrument of sufficient power, with clear and sweet tone, and a fine swell. This church was built to accommodate eighteen hundred persons, but will conveniently hold two thousand, a considerable number of whom, as at the old church, are free; and it is very fully attended. The present clergyman is the Rev. T. Cooke, M.A., a practical and judicious preacher . . . . The tower contains one deep toned bell for the hours, and two small musical ones for the quarters; but the absence of a good ring of bells is to be regretted."[11]

The subsequent alterations make this account a tantalising insight into the original interior décor, but also go a long way in describing the impact the new building had on the town. The reference to "free" places in church concerns the pew renting issue to which we shall return later.

There was some opposition to the name of the church being "St Peter's" as this was thought to be too Roman Catholic. However it was entirely appropriate for a town such as Brighton with such a thriving fishing industry to have a church named after an apostle who had started off as a fisherman. In any case, as we have seen already, the people of Brighton referred to the church as the "New Church", as opposed to the "Old Church"—St Nicholas, which remained as the parish church of the town.

Another description, written a bit later as it mentions King Edward VII and the Prime Minister William Gladstone, but not late enough to include the addition of the chancel that was completed in 1906, read as follows:

> "The church, terminating the northern Steine, has been dedicated to St. Peter. This elegant structure is situated on a triangular piece of ground, formed by the junction of the London and Lewes roads, called the Level. This magnificent church is built of Purbeck[12] stone, and will reflect lasting credit on C. Barry, Esq., the architect who built the Houses of Parliament. Its dimensions are 150 feet from south to north, by about 70 from east to west, and will accommodate about one thousand eight hundred persons.
>
> The tower of the church has long been a landmark at sea and thousands of fisher folk have attended its services. So did Mr Gladstone and King Edward. The building is a parallelogram, with a semi-hexagonal

termination at the north, and a handsome tower at the south end. The style of architecture adopted throughout this church is of the period of Edward the Third, or the highly enriched order of English architecture.

he lower part of the tower, to an equal height with the clerestory of the church, is partly concealed by an outer tower, in three sides of which are large pointed arches, with pedimental canopies, crocketed, and attached pinnacles on each side.

The tower has in each of its faces a pointed doorway and window, and the space between the wall and the tower has a neatly groined roof; the portion which rises above the exterior wall has octagonal buttresses at the angles, ending in similar turrets to those belonging to the outer tower. In each face is a handsome clock dial, and above it a pointed window of two lights, with trefoil heads, and a quatrefoil enclosed in a circle in the sweep of the arch. All these windows are filled with weather boarding.

The finish of the tower is a very elegant pierced battlement, with a small pinnacle in the centre of each face. The east and west sides of the church are divided into five portions, by buttresses of two gradations, which finish above the parapet in very elegant pinnacles, crocketed, and terminating in finials; in each of the divisions is a large pointed window of three lights. Each window has a weather cornice resting on human heads, exquisitely carved.

The clerestory, which ranges with the lower portion of the tower, and has a similar parapet, is made into six divisions by buttresses, without gradations, ending in pinnacles; in each division is a square-headed window of two lights, trefoil heads, and intersecting arches, with a quatrefoil in the centre.

The north end of the aisle has a similar window. Each front of the semi-hexagon, at the north end of the church, is adorned with buttresses, with pointed niches, and pedimental heads rising above the church in rich crocketed pinnacles."

Burton and Sitwell sum up for us the intentions behind Barry's original design, when they say that:

"Barry, as did most of his contemporaries, believed that a Protestant Church should hold its services in an open meeting-room, and he inclined to distrust the Gothic style on the grounds that the dimly lit interior with its elaborate chancels, rood screens and pillared aisles savoured of Popery . . . . St Peter's however represents, in its exterior at least, Barry's conception of a fourteenth century church, and the attempt to apply Middle

Pointed Gothic construction to a Protestant
preaching-house results for the visitor,
in a shock of surprise—far, however, from
unpleasant—as he enters it for the first time."[13]

Even in more modern times, St Peter's is still admired, for
Thomas Cocke, states that "St Peter's cannot fail to be
registered by every visitor to Brighton. It dominates the
view down the valley to the sea, a valley which is still the
central axis of the town."[14]

2. The Building of Brighton Churches

As mentioned earlier, the first incumbent of St Peter's was the Rev Thomas Cooke (1791-1874). He was a close friend of Henry Wagner who had made Cooke one of his curates a year before St Peter's had been opened, and the two of them worked closely together for over forty years. Cooke had a background as a military chaplain during the Napoleonic Wars. He had been in Spain during the last part of the Peninsular War and was present at the Battle of Waterloo.

At either end of the church are memorial tablets to his two wives. His first wife, Jane Finch, died on 8th March 1858 and has a plaque near the south door. This reads, "Jane, eldest daughter of the Hon C. Finch. Beloved wife of Thomas Cooke, M.A. Died 8th March 1858. Also Thomas Cooke, M.A. For forty-five years incumbent of this church who died 18th December 1874 in the 84th year of his age." Interestingly Cooke is referred to here as "incumbent", for he never had the title "vicar" since there was only one vicar in Brighton and that was Wagner. Cooke had been appointed to the "Perpetual Curacy of St Peter's" and so remained a curate for all those forty-five years. As we shall see, St Peter's wasn't to get its own vicar until the later reorganisation.

Despite being widowed in his late sixties, a plaque at the north end of the chancel that was erected in 1901 records that Eliza was his second wife. This one reads, "To the glory of God and in memory of her long connection with this church Eliza C. Cooke—widow of the Rev. T. Cooke, M.A. presented this respond. A.D. 1901. During the first phase of the building reconstruction in the mid 1870's, she also erected the font which stands in the south west corner of the church and dedicated it to her late husband.

Quite a few of the conflicts of the last two hundred years are mentioned in memorials in the interior of St Peter's. The earliest is a memorial tablet by the south door that commemorates a naval officer who died during the Crimea War. It reads, "Sacred to the memory of Richard Onslow Lewis, eldest son of the late Lieut Robert Lewis R.N., Born 5th April 1825. Shipwrecked at Balaklava in the Black Sea while in command of the Resolute 11th November 1854. I commit my soul to the Lord Jesus Christ in the hope of everlasting life." His grandfather was Admiral Sir Richard Onslow, who gained his knighthood after his heroics at the Battle of Camperdown.

Cooke had not two, in the usual way, but three church wardens—one for vicar, one for landsmen and one for fishermen. He was not known to be a brilliant preacher, but he was well respected for his ministry in the town. In order to supplement Christian teaching from the pulpit he instituted a series of evening lectures.[1] Speakers for these included Revd. Berkley Addison, Revd. R. Bracken, Revd. J. Scotland, Revd. J.D. Trigge, Revd. John Julius Hannah (St Peter's' third incumbent) and Revd. J.S.M. Anderson, who later became vicar of St George's, Kemp Town.

Not long into the life of the church the church wardens incurred the displeasure of the parishioners by putting out tenders to add gas lighting to the interior of the church for the evening services. It was felt that such an expense could not be afforded as there were still repayments to be made for the building of the church. There was also an agreement at this time that if the income of the church was ever to exceed £700 per annum, the surplus was going to be devoted to the building of a vicarage in the enclosure at the back of the church. As there is no evidence of any further plans for this, it is assumed that there was never this much left over!

By 1835, the Commissioners for Building New Churches had received £12,000 of the original £15,000 loan, but there was some controversy about the remaining £3,000. It seems that Edward Everard, one of Robert Carr's curates who had become chairman of the New Church Building Committee, had been led to believe that £3,000 of the original loan had been commuted into a grant.[2] This was disputed and the parish Vestry was taken to court for cancelling any further payments. However no evidence could be found to support the parish's case and it was ordered to repay the outstanding amount to the Commissioners for Building New Churches who had brought the case against them.

Henry Michell Wagner, who was to play a key role in the religious life and church development in the town during the mid-nineteenth century, was educated at Eton and King's College Cambridge. However his first visit to Brighton was not a happy experience as he was shot in the hand by a mugger.[3] He took on the task of tutoring the sons of the Duke of Wellington in 1818, before being ordained a deacon in 1821.

Then in 1824 the Duke was authorised to offer him the position of Vicar of Brighton. He knew that Wagner's grandfather, the Rev. Henry Michell, had been Vicar of Brighton from 1744 to 1789, for he, himself, had been a pupil there. This offer prompted Wagner to complete his ordination, which took place four days after he had received it. The original clerestory windows at St Peter's were given by the Wagner family whose initials they bear. "HMW" (Henry Michell Wagner) can clearly be seen on some of them, but there are also other initials which probably belong to other family members.

When William IV became king in 1830, Wagner was presented to him by the Duke of Wellington, who was in his last few months as Prime Minister. When the King came to stay at the Pavilion, Wagner would take services in his private chapel, but on one occasion William IV was annoyed that the bells of St Peter's were not being rung to acknowledge his presence. So Wagner was summoned to the royal presence, but replied that the church bells on Sundays only sounded for the King of Kings. It is said that this reply had the warm approval of Queen Adelaide.[4]

Wagner continued the project that had been started with St Peter's of building new churches in the town which was steadily increasing in population during the middle years of this century, rising from 40,000 in 1841 to 65,000 in 1861. In fact, taking the century as a whole, Carder tells us that the population grew from around 7,000 in 1801 to over 120,000 by 1901.[5] There was also a great need for churches that offered free places for there were only 3,000 free sittings in the town which had an estimated poor population of 18,000.

Between 1834 and 1863, Wagner established six new churches in Brighton. Four of them have since been demolished, and of the two that survive, one is being used as a Greek Orthodox Church. The first of the Wagner's churches was All Souls in Eastern Road. It was opened in 1834, but no longer exists as it was declared redundant and demolished in 1968. His next church was Christ Church in Montpelier Road. This was opened in 1838, but is also no longer with us as it was demolished in 1982.

The third church that he built was St John the Evangelist in Carlton Hill. The area was probably the poorest in Brighton at this time. As with the other churches, Wagner managed to get together a host of benefactors to provide the finance, which in this case included an endowment as there would be no pew rents to support church running costs. It was opened in 1840 but it was declared redundant in 1980. However it avoided demolition as it was sold to the Greek Orthodox community in 1985 and is now the Greek Orthodox Church of the Holy Trinity.

St Paul's in West Street is the most well-known of the Wagner churches in Brighton, and the only one that is still an Anglican Church nowadays—the main threat to its continued existence coming from the Grand Hotel bombing by the I.R.A of October 1984 when the vicar was blown out of his bed.[6] A shorter lived project which barely lasted a century was All Saints, Compton Avenue that was built in 1852, but sadly demolished in 1957. The final Wagner Church was St Anne's in Burlington Street. It was opened in 1863, but it alas went the way of three of its sister churches in 1986 when it, too, was demolished.

Thus by 1864, there were seventeen churches that belonged to the Church of England in Brighton. Wagner's building efforts were not alone, for besides the six churches that he had established, there were eight others that had been opened in the years following his arrival in Brighton in 1824. These were St Mary's (1827), St James' (1828), St George's (1831), St Margaret's (1832), Holy Trinity (1843), St Mark' s (1850), St Stephen's (1852) and St Michael's (1863). All this building reflected the popularity of Christian worship at this time, for this was certainly a high point in the History of the church, as Elleray explains,

> "Statistics provided by the 1851 Census show that Brighton had a total of thirty-eight places of worship, providing 24,035 settings (just over one third of the population).
>
> The typically Victorian fashionable character of nineteenth century church going found in larger towns and cities was also well illustrated in Brighton."[7]

This brief look at church development may seem a diversion from our study of St Peter's, but it does put its story into the context of what was happening in the rest of the town at this time. Of course, besides this, Wagner did have overall responsibility for St Peter's at this time.

The fate of five of Wagner's six churches in the second half of the twentieth century also concerns us as we shall see that St Peter's, itself, was facing a real threat of closure at the beginning of the twenty-first century. The growth of church building during Wagner's time also meant that at the time of his death in 1870, there was still one vicar in Brighton and a host of curates—including Cooke, of course—and there was a need for the structure of the parish of Brighton to be re-organised.

In order to facilitate these changes, Cooke decided to retire in 1872 and resigned the incumbency of St Peter's on 31st March that year. To mark his retirement he was presented with a magnificent silver model of St Peter's Church at a special gathering at the Brighton Pavilion on 8th December.[8] This silver model is currently on display in the Exploring Brighton Gallery, on the ground floor of the Brighton Museum, and Barry's original hexagonal apse that was later demolished can be seen on the right. Underneath the model are inscribed the words:

"A.D. 1873 St PETER'S CHURCH BRIGHTON
Presented to the Rev. Thomas Cooke M.A. as a token of respect and esteem
on his voluntary resignation of the incumbency held by him from
the consecration of the church on 25th January 1828 until 31st October 1873.
AFTER WHICH ST PETER'S BECAME THE PARISH CHURCH OF BRIGHTON"

Cooke was quite frail by this time and was rarely seen in public again. He died in December 1874 at the age of eighty-three.

The Brighton Gazette, reporting his death, said:

> "This week it becomes our melancholy task to describe the death of one who may be described as the "Father of the Brighton Clergy." Incumbent of the Church of St Peter for nearly half a century, and during the whole of that time, and, indeed of his ecclesiastical life, loved, esteemed and honoured by all who had the comfort and pleasure of sharing in his valued friendship. Mr Cooke truly served a long time in the active army of the Church, and served faithfully and earnestly to, being constant in season and out of season in reproving sin, encouraging virtue, exhorting to good works, and above all, preaching the best sermon that can touch the heart by the blameless and eminently consistent life he lived. Receiving his University education at Oriel College, Oxford, he took his degree of M.A., and was ordained priest in 1817. As he continued in active work until 1873, we thus have a total of fifty years during which this devoted servant of God used his best energies to fight the good fight, which we trust will now be rewarded by the Crown of Glory reserved for all who have merited it.

Mr Cooke was a simple hard working parish priest, intent upon the work of His Master, careless of the world's praises so long as his conscience said he acted rightly, anxious not so much for the favour of men as the love of God, working not so industriously after the wealth of this world as for the treasures in Heaven which a store of saved souls will assuredly be laid up for him who has been the privileged means of their salvation. As a preacher Mr Cooke was not what might be called eloquent, in the full acceptance of the term, but his sermons were always characterised by soundness of teaching, plainness of doctrinal truths, carefulness of preparation, and an earnest desire that the talents he had been entrusted with should be employed to the best advantage in that particular field of the Great Vineyard in which he was called upon to labour. His style, too, was polished and easy, and hence his sermons were acceptable to his congregations; and he gained many a success which a man possessed of mere eloquence of expression, without earnestness and piety, would have lacked.

In his parochial ministrations in the extensive district attached to St Peter's, Mr Cooke was equally as successful as he was in the pulpit, and no poor person ever wanted for spiritual or temporal assistance if he knew they required it. Unsparing of both his time and his money, Mr Cooke was a true friend of the poor, as well as a faithful and diligent spiritual guide to his congregation, rich and poor alike."[9]

The Gazette is certainly worth quoting for we can see in these words that St Peter's was more than capably led in its early years by a man well chosen for the task. The longevity of his pastoral role at St Peter's also contrasts markedly with some of his twentieth century successors. It also must be noted that, as we shall see, he was then followed by two equally remarkable men—the Hannahs (father and son)—who brought St Peter's to the forefront of not only the spiritual life of the town but also the secular and civic.

3. The Reorganisation of Brighton Churches

Wagner's successor as Vicar of Brighton was John Hannah. He had been ordained in 1841 and was initially based in Oxford as a private tutor, before becoming rector of the Edinburgh Academy in 1847. He had married Anne Sophia Gregory in 1843 and they stayed at Edinburgh for seven years before moving on to Trinity College Glenalmond in Perthshire in 1854 where he became warden. He had a successful time there, particularly with his work to restore the college's finances.

Thus it was that he came to St Nicholas, Brighton in 1870. Together with the bishop of Chichester, Dr Richard Durnford, he re-organised the whole parish of Brighton. St Nicholas and St Peter's became separate parishes, with St Peter's taking over as the parish church in 1873. Hannah, thus, became vicar of St Peter's, while his son, John Julius Hannah, became vicar of St Nicholas. They all lived together as a family in the St Nicholas' vicarage.

Besides those already mentioned, other new parishes that were set up at this time included St Michael's (1863), St Bartholomew's (1874), St Martin's (1875), The Annunciation (1880), St Matthew's (1883), St Mary Magdalene (1884) and St Luke's (1885). Another important measure was the abolition of the pew system in Brighton and so free and open churches were now up and running. The renting of pews had been a common practice for the raising of income for the church. It was certainly used, as we have seen, to help finance the building of St Peter's.

However the practice had become unpopular during the Victorian period and was gradually being phased out at the time of the reorganisation of the Brighton parishes.

By this time there were three Sunday services at St Peter's. At eleven o'clock there was the morning service with sermon and a celebration of the Holy Communion. Then there was evening prayer with sermon at half past three and evening prayer with sermon at seven o'clock. There was also a celebration of Holy Communion at eight o'clock in the morning on the first Sunday in the month.[1]

St Paul's had been opened in 1848 by Henry Wagner whose son, Arthur Henry Wagner, became its first incumbent. He stayed there till his death in 1902, but during his time St Paul's was at the forefront of the Anglo-Catholic Revival of the Victorian period. There was an infamous case that involved Constance Kent who had murdered her half-brother in 1860. When the case came to trial Arthur Wagner refused to give evidence that she had disclosed to him during confession. This provoked uproar in the town, as "confession" was seen as a catholic practice, and there were even calls for a House of Commons Select Committee to look into the style of worship at St Paul's.

There were a number of curates serving under Wagner whose "ritualistic" practices were much criticised, such as Charles Beanlands and John Purchas. However it was when two more of these curates—E. Grindle and P.N. Willis—left the Church of England to become Roman Catholics that things came to head with a demonstration in Brighton against the confessional—as practised at St

Paul's. As a result a public meeting was held at the Dome which resolved unanimously to "resist every effort to bring into our Protestant Church practices which are contrary to God's Word." There was a packed house, but one notable absentee was the Vicar of Brighton, Dr Hannah himself. This was probably a wise move under these extraordinary circumstances.

Meanwhile Dr Hannah was able to extend his sphere of influence well outside the life of the churches of Brighton. For example, it was reported in the Brighton Argus that he:

> "took a keen interest in promoting emigration; and in May 1871, when a number of children were about to take their departure from Brighton to Canada, he delivered a most impressive address to the children at the Town Hall. There were sixty-six boys and eleven girls sent out under the auspices of the Juvenile Emigration Society; and the Vicar presented each one with a Bible and Prayer Book as they left for their new homes."[2]

Although this brings to light an often hidden element in the treatment of orphaned children, it does also show that Hannah, as a church leader, was prepared to minister to all parts of society including the disadvantaged young.

For another area that concerned John Hannah was education, since he had moved south from a teaching position in Scotland when he became vicar of Brighton. He became chairman of the first School Board in Brighton. These Board Schools had been set up by Forster's Education Act of 1870 in order to provide universal primary education. The school boards were elected locally and managed the finances, building and running of schools in their area.

He was also involved with Brighton College, which had been founded in 1845. He was chairman of the board of governors there for a period in 1873, but continued to support the work of the college as a vice-patron and vice-President. As well as this he was President of the Committee of Management of the Chichester Diocesan Training College for Schoolmistresses, Vice-President of the Brighton Parliamentary and Literary Society, Vice-President of the Central Brighton Church Sunday School Association, Chairman of the Brighton, Hove and Preston Charity Organisation and a Life Member of the Sussex Archaeological Society, in which he took a keen interest.

But, returning to events surrounding St Peter's, on 21st May 1874 there was a very important vestry meeting that was held at Brighton Town Hall. There were three issues under discussion:

1) To consider the propriety of making certain alterations and enlargements to St Peter's Church.

2) To facilitate these alterations with voluntary contributions and by obtaining the necessary faculty.

3) To achieve as a result a "more commodious and appropriate" setting for the parish church of Brighton.

It is at this point that the Somers Clarkes come into the story of St Peter's. Somers Clarke senior, had been Henry Wagner's solicitor and was clerk to the vestry—a position he had held since 1830. It was his nephew, Somers Clarke junior, who was going to be responsible for the building of the chancel at the north end of the church. He had been a pupil of Sir Gilbert Scott, and had already, at the behest of Henry Wagner's sons, been the architect of St Martin's Church in Lewes Road.

Somers Clarke had produced a survey of St Peter's, showing that the building, fifty years on from its foundation, was still sound although there was some erosion to the external pinnacles. However he reported that the church had no chancel and was extremely short for its width. The need for a chancel probably stemmed from the Oxford Movement that was prevalent at this time. This was marked by a desire to return the Church of England to embrace some of the Roman Catholic traditions that had been swept away at the time of the Protestant Reformation.

Many older churches had chancels, but St Peter's' original design had embraced the plain form that Protestant practice had actively encouraged. There was certainly a clear difference between St Peter's and some of the Wagner churches in the town, such as St Paul's whose websites states "It was built by Richard Cromwell Carpenter in the true spirit of the Oxford Movement and the Gothic Revival. While Saint Peter's had gothic decoration, Saint Paul's was built with newly researched gothic proportions, structures and symbolism." [3]

As a result Barry's semi-hexagonal apse at the front of the church was under threat, but Somers Clarke also went on to criticise the galleries as a mass exodus from them in the event of a fire would be most hazardous. He then pointed out that six hundred members of the congregation had no space to kneel in this area of the church.

It was Somers Clarke senior, as clerk to the vestry, who presented the remedies, proposed in the report, which were as follows:

1) The building of a new chancel
2) The restoration of a chancel screen
3) The removal of the south gallery and organ
4) Reseating the east and west galleries, and providing independent staircases for them
5) Adding one bay to the nave
6) Boarding the roof with oak
7) Building a turret staircase

The cost for this work was estimated at £16,000, but the alterations would result in comfortable accommodation for 1,614 people. A modified version of this plan was also prepared with a costing of £3,000, while the very minimum cost would be £1,320 for minor alterations that were urgently needed.

The Brighton Herald, reporting the Somers Clarke's proposals, added:

> "Referring to the position of the Cathedral, unfortunately placed in a small town at a remote extremity of the Diocese, the report stated that the Parish Church of Brighton should be well able to accommodate larger numbers of persons than any other Parish Church in the County on the occasions of ordinations, visitations and the like, which the importance and central position of the town must often lead to being held here. Choral Festivals were also more easily attended in Brighton than elsewhere in the County. These objects could not be obtained without a building of considerable capacity, not only in the nave for the people, but in the chancel for the clergy and choir; fully justifying the proposal to add considerably to the length of the present building, and as much as means would permit, to increase its magnificence."[4]

Dr Hannah was quoted as saying that he did not want to turn St Peter's into a cathedral, but a model of what a parish church should be. He said there were other places with cathedral-like churches, such as Yarmouth and Leeds, but "which were neither cathedrals in reality nor in name, but were edifices worthy of being mother-churches of their respective towns." However he was mindful that as vicar of Brighton he did have responsibility for other churches in the town and he could not neglect their needs by putting disproportionate resources into developing St Peter's.

It fell to Mr H.T. West to move the following resolution, "That St Peter's Church being now the Parish Church of Brighton, it is necessary that it should be altered and enlarged so as to fit it for the Parish Church of this large and populous town in the centre of the county, in accordance with the report and plans now submitted to the Vestry, the same being carried out by voluntary contributions." In moving the motion he added, among other things, that Brightonians "took a pride in their town, in their Corporation, and they prided themselves upon their Esplanade, their Cricket Ground, their Volunteers, and why should they not take a pride in their Parish Church?"[5]

He concluded by adding, "Besides having a Parish Church worthy to represent Christianity in the town of Brighton . . . . part of the scheme was to afford accommodation according to the wants of the times, and to make the Churches the poor man's Churches as well as the rich man's Churches, and to do away with the obnoxious arrangement of hired sittings for the rich and others for the poor."

Mr Lawrence Coppard seconded the resolution, trusting that the generosity of the parishioners would eclipse the caution that the vicar was showing towards the necessary expenditure. He continued, "Brighton was a noble town; they could boast of their Aquarium, the Pavilion, and they could say they had In Brighton what no other town in England, or even in Europe, had so far as various matters required for the accommodation of visitors went. He for one was a great advocate for a good Church, and thought their parish church should be something that should eclipse most of the Churches in the county."

He continued by saying that it had always occurred to his mind that St Peter's was a Church very short indeed for that style of building, and that by lengthening it they would give it very great importance and beauty to it. He spoke in favour of the Church being made "commodious and comfortable . . . . so that worshippers going there might go away perfectly satisfied that they had no annoyance in going there and that they enjoyed their worship without the slightest inconvenience"

The meeting is reported as being very much in favour of adopting the larger scheme, although the vicar was disinclined to try to raise £16,000 by public subscription. As the discussion moved on The Rev J.H. North, the incumbent of St George's backed other speakers who said that the resolution should be worded so as to carry out the larger scheme. There was much vocal support for the measures in question, and the vicar was at one point accused of being "fainthearted"

If there was one characteristic Dr Hannah did not have, it was certainly faintheartedness. It is suspected that his caution was due to the weight of his responsibilities in the matter, but his mind, at this point, was swayed by the commitment that many of the speakers showed for the scheme. This gave him the encouragement that many were prepared to back the proposals and so he offered a donation of £1,000, payable in instalments, towards the cost of the work.

A Building Committee was appointed by this meeting. It consisted of the Vicar, the Mayor, the Churchwardens, the Overseeers of Brighton, Montague Scott (M.P. for Eastern Sussex), James Lloyd Ashbury (M.P. for Brighton), Sir John Cordy Burrows (whose statue stands in the Old Steine), H. Verrall, Alderman Martin, F. Hayllar, W. Marchant, G. Lynn and all subscribers of £50 to the Fund. Its remit was, according to the Brighton Herald, to "aid in carrying out the alteration and enlargement of St Peter's Church, and obtain funds for that purpose."

However no real chancel was to be built for another twenty-five years, for this was going to prove the greater part of all the proposed alterations to the original church. So the second plan was carried out and after its completion, the church was re-opened on Easter Sunday, 16th April, 1876. The antiquated pews had been replaced by wooden open oak benches and the old fashioned stoves had been removed with "heating apparatus of a modern type" put in their place.

The original organ by Lincoln in the south gallery was removed in 1874 and space was found in the west gallery for a restored and enlarged version that was re-opened on 30th September 1877. This was later sold to St Paul's Church in St Albans. Temporary vestries had been built and a new reredos of Caen stone and alabaster with canopied niches, designed by E.L. Blackburne, was inserted by J.W. Searle of Walworth in the place of Barry's original screen in 1877.[6] A new font was also installed in the south west corner, which, as mentioned earlier, was given by Mrs Cooke as a memorial to her husband.

On Sunday 28th May 1876, the bishop of Chichester preached at the formal reopening of the church. However Dr Hannah was not completely satisfied with the changes as it is said that he still wanted:

- A new pulpit
- A more commodious vestry for choir and clergy
- Improvements to the seating in the gallery
- Improvements to the gallery staircases
- Painted glass in the side windows of the church. Hannah wanted these modelled on the Old Testament "Heroes of Faith" from Hebrews 11.

These changes were going to have to wait to be implemented till the incumbency of his son, John Julius Hannah, although there were already a number of stained-glass windows designed by Charles Earmer Kempe (a relative of Thomas Read Kemp) of Old Place, Lindfield.

In 1876 Hannah became archdeacon of Lewes. He kept this position until his death, but he resigned as Vicar of Brighton in 1887. The Brighton Herald of 29th April 1876 reported:

> "The friends and parishioners of Dr Hannah will doubtless be gratified by the following announcement,

"The Rev. Dr Hannah, Vicar of Brighton, has been offered, and has accepted, the Archdeaconry of Lewes, vacated by the death of the Venerable W.B. Otter."

The Rev. Dr Hannah has not long been in Sussex—since his appointment to the Vicarage of Brighton 5· years ago, and his selection for the office of Archdeacon of Lewes is an honourable proof that he has gained the confidence of those in authority."

He is also well described by the Brighton Gazette:

"Dr Hannah will long live in the memory of the people of Brighton, and indeed his name widespread now. We will not speak of the energy he has displayed in forwarding the education of the parishioners, of the noble efforts he has made to break the bands of exclusiveness and to throw open the Churches to the poor, of the peculiar tact and care he has taken in in filling up the appointments which have come under his patronage, of the ready sympathy, earnest kindliness and courteous geniality which made him endeared to the hearts of all members of his large flock. He is truly an earnest Christian gentleman. As a preacher he possesses considerable eloquence . . . . which adds considerably to the instructiveness and usefulness of his sermons."[7]

John Hannah died on 1st June 1888. The following day, the Brighton Argus reported:

> "During the seventeen years over which his control extended, he was able to effect great and important changes: many of which although opposed at first, have since been admitted to be not only alterations but improvements. The contrast between the churches of Brighton at the beginning and at the close of his active work in the town must have been particularly gratifying to a churchman such as Dr Hannah, while the changes he inaugurated will undoubtedly have an important bearing on the whole future religious History of Brighton.
>
> Dr Hannah at first startled his parishioners by what seemed to many an old Brightonian not only a revolutionary but almost a sacrilegious proposal of making St Peter's Church the religious centre of the town instead of the Church of St Nicholas . . . . Still as time went on and the people of Brighton generally saw the tact and patience with which Dr Hannah pursued the task, they could not fail to feel respect for their new Vicar. It is not necessary to analyse minutely the constituent elements that contributed to the popularity which Dr Hannah enjoyed throughout his period of residence in Brighton. His reputation for scholarship scored him in good stead, his deep sympathy with the young, his invariable

courtesy, his great ability as a public speaker, his skill in debate, his cheerfulness and smartness in repartee, may all be mentioned in contributing their share; but perhaps his breadth of view, and his earnest devotion to the welfare and enlargement of the Church of England, did more than anything to call forth the admiration and respect of his fellow townsmen and co-religionists."[8]

Further on in the article, the Argus reveals the popularity of church attendance during his time, which obviously helped towards the church building and development programmes that were going on, when it says:

"Dr Hannah proved his attractiveness as a preacher by filling the Church of St Nicholas to its utmost capacity while ministering there until 1873, and in the larger building, St Peter's, the same success attended him."

John and Anna Hannah both have memorials in the church. There is a window on the east side of the church that bears the inscription, "To the glory of God and the honour the memory of Anne Sophia wife of John Hannah, Vicar of Brighton. She died 25th February 1876 in the 59th year of her age." John Hannah's memorial marble plaque is set just to the left of this window by the east door.

It reads,

"In the Parochial Cemetery
Lies all that can die of the

Venerable John Hannah D.C.L. Oxon.,
Fellow of Lincoln College, Oxford 1840-1844
Chaplain of Coombe Lonca, Oxon 1843-1845,
Rector of Edinburgh Academy 1847-1854,
Warden of Trinity College Clenalmond,
And Pantonian Professor of Theology
1854-1870
Bampton Lecturer 1863,
Vicar of Brighton and Rector of West
Blatchington 1870-1887,
Prebendary of Sidlesham in Chichester
Cathedral 1874-1888,
Archdeacon of Lewes 1876-1888

Born at Lincoln 16th July 1818
Died at the Vicarage Brighton 1st June 1888

He divided the parish of Brighton into
ecclesiastical districts,
Making each district church free and
unappropriated for ever
He transferred the parochial rights of the
parish of Brighton
From the old church of St Nicholas to this building.
Which he greatly beautified and improved.

This commemorative tablet was placed here
by his only son
Who succeeded him as Vicar of Brighton

"They rest from their labours,
And their works do follow them"

That last quotation comes from Revelation 14, verse 13. The tablet also reminds us that the vicars of Brighton also had the old medieval church of West Blatchington to look after from 1744-1940. It is also called St Peter's and the village of West Blatchington was absorbed into the Borough of Hove in 1928.

4. The Addition of the Chancel

John Hannah was succeeded by his son, the Rev John Julius Hannah (1845-1931). He had been educated at Trinity College, Glenalmond and Balliol College, Oxford, and trained for the Church of England ministry at Ripon College, Cuddesdon. He began his career as a curate at St Mary's Brill in Buckinghamshire, before coming to Brighton to take over the parish of St Nicholas from his father in 1873. He moved to St Peter's at Christmas 1887.

At this stage there was a growing determination to bring about more changes to the building; in particular the proposals for a new chancel were certainly gathering momentum. The opening of St Bartholomew's—the imposing "Noah's Ark" building just up the London Road from St Peter's—had probably increased the desire for these changes. They were certainly something the new vicar was determined to see through as he began his incumbency at St Peter's. A letter was produced which detailed the proposals, as well as requesting financial assistance in funding the scheme. It read as follows:-

"Dear Sir or Madam

When it became necessary to sub-divide the enormous parish of Brighton after the death of the Rev. H.M. Wagner, who for forty-seven years had been Vicar of the Undivided Parish, Archdeacon Hannah, the then Vicar of Brighton, submitted a scheme by which he thought the desired object could be carried into effect. This involved constituting the Church of St Peter the Mother Chapel of the town, and he then advocated three great objects which he laid before the Parishioners.

The first of these was to enlarge and build a chancel for the New Parish Church; the second to provide endowments for the District Churches; and the third to build at least two new churches in the more neglected portions of the town.

Owing to the more pressing nature of the two latter proposals, they have been taken in hand and completed first. But now that no great scheme of Church extension is before the Public in the Parish of Brighton, it seems to many of the Parishioners that the time has now come when something ought to be done to make the Parish church more worthy of the position it has been called upon to occupy.

Accordingly a public meeting was held in the Pavilion to consider this question on Thursday 26th April (1888). Viscount Hampden, Lord Lieutenant of the County presided, and after a full explanation from the Vicar of Brighton as to the details of the scheme, the following resolution, proposed by the Rt. Hon. W.T. Marriott M.P. and seconded by the Venerable Archdeacon of Lewes, was carried unanimously.

That this meeting, having heard the statements of the vicar of Brighton and the Architect, is of the opinion that the time has now come when a rigorous effort should be made to raise the funds by voluntary contributions to carry out the enlargement of the Parish Church, on the general lines which were approved by the Vestry in 1874 (a reference to the meeting at the Town hall on 21st May 1874), and to introduce such other improvements into the fabric as may make it more suitable to be the Mother Church of this large and populous Parish."

The building committee was thereupon appointed and the Executive Committee has since been chosen, and this committee now appeals very urgently to all the Parishioners of Brighton, as also to the regular visitors, to place the funds at their disposal to enable them to carry out so useful, so important and so necessary a work.

The scheme has the warmest approval and support of the Lord Bishop of the Diocese, as the following letter addressed to the Vicar of Brighton will show.

Tuesday 24th April 1888

"MY DEAR VICAR—

I am sorry that my engagements in London, our convocation being now sitting, prevent my attending the Meeting on Thursday for I heartily approve the purpose for which it has been called.

This is to make St Peter's Church worthy of the great town of Brighton so that it may hold its proper place both as to the dignity of architecture and convenient accommodation of the large congregation for those whose it is designed.

For whatever be the claims of other Churches, it is not to be forgotten that St Peter's is legally and actually the Parish Church of Brighton. It has attached to it the far biggest district in the town and the most numerous population.

Your father determined wisely when he transferred the title of Parish Church for St Nicholas to St Peter's, and I trust a blessing will rest on your endeavours to perfect the work which he began.

As a token of my full approbation and earnest wishes for your success, I beg leave to add £50 to the subscriptions which I conclude will this day be set on foot.

sincerely yours
R. CICESTER"

The leaflet[1] went on to outline the advantages of the proposed changes:

1. Brighton will gain with a Mother Church fit to take its proper place both as to the dignity of architecture and convenient accommodation of the large congregation for whose use it is intended.
2. The building will be made worthy of the splendid site which it occupies.
3. The Church will be provided with a Chancel, which at present it does not possess, but for which there is great need, as at present the very inadequate arrangements for the large voluntary choir are made at the sacrifice of a considerable portion of the area of the Church.
4. Room will be made for 333 additional worshippers in the Body of the Church.
5. Proper vestry accommodation will be provided which at present the Church is entirely without.
6. A fireproof Muniment Room will be provided for the safe custody of the Registers of Brighton, which at present have to be kept at various places, for want of accommodation.
7. A Church Room will be constructed which will serve for classes, choir practice, signing the registers at weddings, and which will also be available for all sorts of Church Meetings such as Chapters of the Clergy, Meetings of the Diocesan Society, etc. at present all such meetings have to be held at a hired room at the Pavilion.
8. Adequate means for heating the building will be supplied. At present there is nothing of the kind,

and the want was severely felt during the last winter.

Then came the "bottom line" as all this work needed to be paid for. The addition of the chancel is certainly a testament to the prosperity of late Victorian Brighton, as it was completed entirely by donations. The leaflet went on:

> "To complete all that is sketched out, will cost probably not far short of twenty thousand pounds. But it is proposed to proceed with the work by sections. The committee are very anxious to have in hand at least three thousand ponds in the course of the next few weeks in order that the building foundations for the rooms under the chancel may be proceeded with early in the Spring.
>
> Signed on behalf of and by order of the committee,
> John Julius Hannah, Vicar of Brighton
> Gordon Cavenagh   )
> William Bennett   ) churchwardens
> Charles E. Hill   )
> G. Somers Clarke, Hon. Sec."

It was the latter—Somers Clarke—the same architect that had produced the previous plans who was to design the new construction. He was now in partnership with John Thomas Micklethwaite who had also been a pupil of Sir

Gilbert Scott. In the crypt at St Peter's there is a tablet on the wall which reads as follows:—

"These vestries were added to the Parish Church of Brighton—1889

John Julius Hannah, Vicar of Brighton

G. Cavenagh   )
W. Bennett   ) churchwardens
W. Botting   )
Somers Clarke, Architect
Geo. Lynn & Sons, Builders
T. Shelmerdine, Clerk of the Works
R.J. Burdon   )
Heathcote Smith   )
Cecil Deedes   ) curates
W. Carr Selby   )
W.T.Dutton   )
Wilmot Philips   )
W. Robinson—verger

This tablet is the gift of Mr Churchwarden Bennett"

However before the chancel was built, the initial work was carried out on a lady chapel to the east of it which had now come into the scheme of things. The window was designed by Charles Earmer Kempe—as was the main one at the head of the chancel later on. It depicts the crucifixion, the ascent to Calvary and St Veronica's Act of Devotion. Kempe was a Sussex man who lived in Lindfield for a while and is buried in the churchyard at

Ovingdean. Bishop Durnford laid the foundation stone for this in 1889, and its construction was finished in 1898. The inscription on the foundation stone reads:

"Dedicating this work to the Glory of God, the stone is laid by Richard, Lord Bishop of Chichester MDCCCXXXIX"

There is now no trace of the original foundation stone which had been laid back in 1824, for it was probably sited on the outside of the hexagonal apse that Sir Charles Barry had designed at the north end (liturgical east) of the church. It is suspected that it was removed when the chancel extension was added, and the apse was demolished.

There is a Latin inscription on one of the pillars to the bishop, who died in 1890, and was surely a good friend to St Peter's during this preliminary period of building reconstruction. It reads, "In Piam Memoriam Ricardi Durnford Episcopi Cicestrensis Qui Annos Amplius XXV Pavit Suos In Innocentia Cordis Sui," a rough translation of which would be "In reverent memory of Richard Durnford, Bishop of Chichester, who fed his flock for more than twenty-five years in the innocence of his heart." One of the houses at Brighton College is named after him.

On another pillar on the west side of the chancel is a memorial to William, the son of John Julius Hannah. He was killed in South Africa on 21st October 1899 when his camp came under enemy bombardment. The inscription reads, "In loving memory of William Maitland Julius

Hannah, Lieut. Leicestershire Regiment, killed in action while gallantly fighting for his country near Glencoe, South Africa, in the Boer War 1899. His sorrowing friends in Brighton have built this pulpit by public subscription." The pulpit that was constructed along with the new chancel was also dedicated to him with the Latin inscription, "Filii Dilectissimi" (to a most beloved son).

Not long after Hannah had received the news about the death of his son, there was a meeting called to promote the enrolment of volunteers for the fighting. As it was his duty as honorary chaplain to the Brighton volunteer forces, he bravely went on the platform to "exhort other fathers to do as he had done." The Brighton & Hove Herald continues, "The brave solemnity of his words will never be forgotten by those who heard them."[2]

Another member of the family is commemorated in a window on the west side of the church just to the left of the door that leads through to the church hall. In the centrepiece is inscribed the words from Luke 5, verse 10, "Fear not from henceforth thou shalt catch men." On the bottom left hand corner it says, "This window was dedicated on the feast of St Peter 1909 in grateful memory of Annie Barbara, wife of John Julius Hannah, Vicar of Brighton 1888-1902 and Dean of Chichester who died 10th May 1907." St Peter's seems to be full of memorials to the wives of the incumbents, but it is a good reminder of the important role that they have played (and continue to play) in the life of a church.

Dale sums up the effect that the building of the new chancel had on the church when he tells us that:

"At the same time as the chancel was added, the three galleries were removed from the nave. With their removal, the atmosphere of the church passed from the eighteenth to the nineteenth centuries."[3]

By the time the new chancel was completed in 1906, John Julius Hannah had moved on. He was appointed Dean of Chichester in 1902, and served there for twenty-seven years before retiring in 1929. He died on 1st June 1931, the anniversary of his father's death, at his home in West Hoathly. The Brighton & Hove Herald spoke warmly about him and the effect his life had had not just in Brighton but throughout the county of Sussex.

"It is hardly too much to say that for close upon half a century The Rev. John Julius Hannah, sometime Vicar of Brighton and afterwards Dean of Chichester was the outstanding clerical personality in Sussex. With his commanding presence and his general humanity he moved through parish, through Cathedral and through the Diocese with the force of some invigorating gale from the sea.

Robust in person, robust in opinions, blessed with a sanctified common sense, he swept all before him, all stiffness, cant and misunderstanding. Essentially the administrator, a manager of men and of methods, he never left a committee room or a public meeting without making its members

feel in better humour than when he entered.
He was not only the breeze. He was also the
sunshine. He swept away only to make grow.
Laughter and sanity followed in his train.

He was an incorrigible and infectious
optimist.[4] Nothing daunted him, whether the
long-delayed completion of the Brighton
Parish Church, the difficulties of the Diocese
and Cathedral, or even the state of the
Church of England . . . . The fact was that
no other Churchman, and for that matter,
no other layman could compete with The
Rev. John Julius Hannah in affectionate
widely-spread popularity. He appealed
straight to the heart of all men."

Hannah was certainly an energetic Vicar of Brighton
during his time there. He was described as having
remarkable individual gifts and was certainly a fine
specimen of muscular Christianity. As Brighton
developed in these latter years of the nineteenth
century, Hannah, through his vigour, raised the status
of the "Vicar of Brighton" in such a way as it became a
position of outstanding importance, not only in the
religious life of the town but also in all its social and civic
activities. He is said to have looked after everything in
the town with "genial and good humoured autocracy."

The following quotation seems to typify the man. "Crisis
in the Church! I have never known a time when there was
not a crisis in the Church. I hope never to know a time
when there is no crisis. As long as the Church of England

is the Church of Christ, and as long as it is in the world, there is bound to be a crisis following crisis."[5] He was of the strong belief, according to Alfred Rose, the Vicar of Brighton at the time of his death, "that the Church should identify itself with the life of the town, and he threw himself vigorously into every movement which he hoped and believed made for progress, and as resolutely opposed what he felt was wrong."

John Julius Hannah was succeeded as Vicar of Brighton by Benedict George Hoskyns in 1902. He was born in 1856, and was educated at Bradfield, Haileybury and Jesus College Cambridge. He rowed for Cambridge in the 1877 Boat Race—which was the only dead heat in the race's History! After his ordination in 1880, he was a curate at St Mary's Southampton, before moving on to be vicar at St Denys in the same city in 1888. He then became a canon at Truro Cathedral in 1895.

The Brighton and Hove Herald speaks of him as being totally different from his predecessor. He was rather reserved and sensitive, but had deep sympathies for the people of his parish. As a result "Both he and his wife, a lady of engaging charm and tact, won for themselves a real place in the hearts of their parish and were held in affection and reverence." It also says, concerning his role as Vicar of Brighton, that "he was held in the utmost honour in the town as a man who by character and attainments fully upheld the high traditions associated with that important office"[6]

The most important event of his fifteen years at St Peter's was the completion of the chancel in 1906. One of the glories of the new addition to the parish church was the magnificent window to the north (liturgical east) that was dedicated to the late Queen Victoria, with the words, "Giving thanks to Almighty God, the King of Kings, for the happy reign of Victoria, for 63 years Queen of these realms, the people of Brighton dedicate this window to His glory and for the adornment of this church." The window was designed by Charles Earmer Kempe, and shows Jesus in glory surrounded by His saints, with an image of the Queen that clearly be seen in the bottom right-hand corner.

The chancel was consecrated on 29th June 1906 (the Feast of St Peter) by Ernest Wilberforce, Lord Bishop of Chichester, in the presence of the Archbishop of Canterbury, Randall Davidson. Under the Headline, "The Archbishop of Canterbury in Brighton," the Sussex Daily News reported the following day,

> "So much has already been said, over a long period of years, about the efforts which have been made to complete the Brighton Parish Church that many people will learn with a sense of thankful relief that the building has at last been supplied with the chancel which was designed for it from the beginning. It is a chancel of noble proportions, higher than the nave, and certainly fairer to look upon, though this contrast may not be so noticeable when the rest of the church has been renovated. All the galleries have been swept away, and the interior now has a much more stately and imposing appearance . . . . The

nave of the Parish Church is still rather dingy and it may be hoped that funds will presently be forthcoming to bring it into harmony with the chancel. The church will then have an architectural grandeur worthy of its great purpose and the town.

The stage which has been reached is, however, a striking testimony to the persistence of the Dean of Chichester during the many years of his work as Vicar of Brighton, and to the unceasing efforts and generous financial support of his successor, Canon Hoskyns, in coping with the task that devolved upon him. How thoroughly St Peter's has entered into the life of Brighton was seen once more yesterday in the large congregation which assembled for the consecration of the chancel and the side chapel by the Bishop of Chichester and the Archbishop of Canterbury. . . . . The widespread interest in the event was shown by the assembly of large numbers of people around the enclosures of the church, and there was some lamentation among the spectators that it was not possible to get into even the grounds, which were closed to all but ticket-holders."[7]

The services began that day with a 7.30 Holy Communion with about 900 communicants. Then the main service of the day began at 11.30 with the Mayor and Corporation in attendance as well as those who had acquired tickets for the occasion. The intended procession around the church singing the hymn "The Church's One Foundation" had to be abandoned due to heavy rain. Nevertheless the procession that entered the church was indeed splendid. The Archbishop and Bishop, accompanied by a selection of assorted clergy, alongside the augmented choirs, commenced the ceremony in an inspiring way. The service continued with a mixture of religious rites and the obligatory legal requirements as the Bishop conducted the consecration before the Archbishop gave the sermon.

Randall Davidson was the longest holder of the post of Archbishop of Canterbury since the Reformation and the first Archbishop to retire—all his predecessors having died in office. His sermon was taken from Acts 28:15, "When Paul saw the brethren he thanked God and took courage." His message was that in looking round at a great congregation in such a magnificent new building; there is every encouragement to take courage for the tasks ahead. He went on to say, "It fills the soul with thoughts as to what will the work which may here be accomplished for the bettering of peoples' lives when, say, 100 years shall have passed over these new laid stones, and when that chancel pavement shall be trodden by the feet of thousands who are yet unborn."

After the service was over there was a lunch in the Banqueting Room of the Royal Pavilion. The Mayor gave a speech, proposing a toast to "The Parish of Brighton", giving particular praise to the vicar and his predecessor, whose wholehearted efforts had made this particular day possible. The Bishop replied, before Canon Hoskyns took the floor to express his thanks. He thanked the Dean of Chichester (his predecessor, John Julius Hannah), the architects (Somers Clarke and Micklethwaite), the builders (Norman & Burt—and prior to them, Messrs Lynn), Mr Bailey, the clerk of works, Mr Kempe (who had created the magnificent east window), the workmen (who had completed their task without a single accident), and last but certainly not least all the people of Brighton who had given financial support to the project.

There were further speeches from various others who included the Archbishop for whom this was the first visit to Brighton. He drew laughter as he expressed a desire to see if the sea front was all it was made out to be. The final words, though, fittingly belonged to Dean Hannah. As he rose to his feet there was a large round of applause, and he was able to profess gratitude that, "After all the many years of work, and after all the disappointments and delays that have taken place, at last in God's good time this great work on which we have worked for so long has been brought this day to a happy and full completion."

There were more additions subsequent to the completion of the chancel, for in 1910 an organ was installed in memory of King Edward VII. This has been called "one of St Peter's greatest treasures," for it is a superb example of the work of "Father" Henry Willis which was built in 1888 and originally installed in the Hampstead Conservatoire. It contains four manuals and forty-three speaking stops and is regarded as one of the finest unaltered Willis organs of cathedral dimensions.[8] The case that surrounds the organ is much more modern, being added during a restoration in 1966. Such is the quality of this organ that it is said that at one time even King's College Cambridge wanted to purchase it

Edward VII had been a frequent visitor to Brighton and Hove, finding the sea air good for his health. The Peace Statue which stands on the sea front on the boundary between Brighton and Hove was erected in his memory. His funeral took place at Windsor on Friday 20th May 1910. It speaks volumes for his popularity among the people that St Peter's must have been one among many churches that marked the occasion by holding services themselves as well. The church was packed for the occasion, and it was followed by a further ceremony on the lawns outside the church which was attended by 10,000 people with a full choir and both the Mayor and the Vicar speaking.

Then in 1914 ten bells, which were said to be the largest in Sussex were donated by John Thornton Richman of Lewes. They were cast by Mears and Stainbank at the Whitechapel Foundry, famous for its cast of Big Ben over half a century earlier, and were dedicated on 14th April. Two bells had originally been given by St Nicholas Church in 1828, and these had been added to by eight new ones, all bearing the name of J. Warner & Son, in 1882. These were all replaced in 1914 and St Peter's was now said to have the largest bells in the county. The heaviest is the tenor bell which weighs 25· hundredweights. They were hung in a cast iron frame on two levels, the treble, second and ninth being hung above the others. Certainly they ring out loud and clear on a Sunday morning!

However the bells became silent in the August of that year. On the first Sunday after the declaration of war, 9th August, there was an immense congregation. A special intercession took place and daily intercessions were then started with the names of those from the parish who were serving their country being read out and large numbers attending.

Sir Charles Barry (1795 -1860)

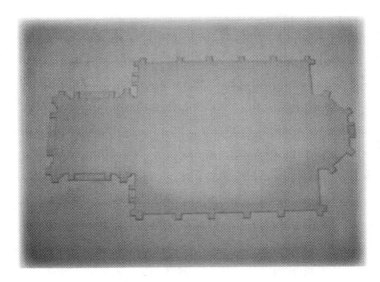

Plan of the original church

Original Church Interior Liturgical East End

Original Church Interor Liturgical West End

Thomas Cooke, Curate at St Peter's, 1828-1873

Church Model, given to Thomas Cooke, now in
Brghton Museum

THE VENERABLE JOHN HANNAH, D.C.L.
VICAR OF BRIGHTON 1870-87
ARCHDEACON OF LEWES 1876-88

John Hannah, Vicar of St Peter's, 1873-1887

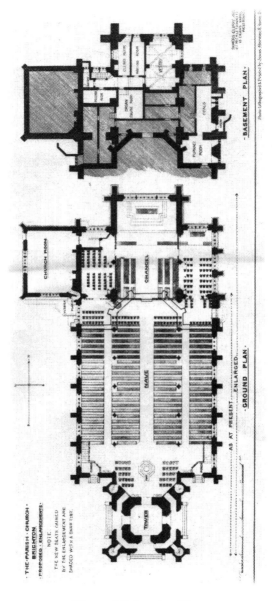

Chancel Extension Plans

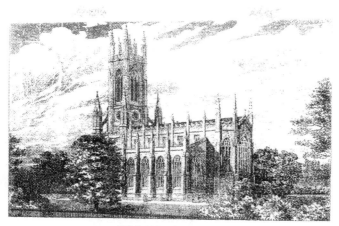

THE CHURCH AS IT NOW IS.

THE CHURCH ENLARGED

Church Extension Drawings

JOHN JULIUS HANNAH, D.D.
VICAR OF BRIGHTON 1888-1902
DEAN OF CHICHESTER 1902-29

John Julius Hannah, Vicar of St Peter's, 188-1902

CANON BENEDICT GEORGE HOSKYNS, M.A.
VICAR OF BRIGHTON 1902-1917
ARCHDEACON OF HASTINGS 1917-1920
ARCHDEACON OF CHICHESTER 1920-1934

Benedict Hoskyns, Vicar of St Peter's, 1902-1917

CANON F. DORMER PIERCE, B.A.
VICAR OF BRIGHTON 1917-23

Francis Dormer Pierce, Vicar of St Peter's, 1917-1923

The Grave of Francis Dormer Pierce at
West Blatchington Church

CANON FREDERICK CYRIL NUGENT HICKS, D.D.
VICAR OF BRIGHTON 1924-27
BISHOP OF GIBRALTAR 1927-33
BISHOP OF LINCOLN 1933-42

Frederick Hicks, Vicar of St Peter's, 1924-1927

The original reredos in the chancel of St Peter's, later destroyed by fire

Liturgical East window showing the restoration of the area around the altar after the fire

After the reopening the south end was unsafe, nets were in place to catch falling plaster, but the congregation enjoyed a cup of coffee in this area after the service.

St Peter's in the 21st Century

5. St Peter's in the Twentieth Century

Hoskyns became Archdeacon of Hastings in 1915, and resigned as Vicar of Brighton in 1917. According to the church service book, he had been ill and unable to officiate at services prior to his retirement. He moved to Chichester in 1920 to become Archdeacon there and retired in 1934. He died at Winchester on 11th September 1935.

He was succeeded at St Peter's by Francis Dormer Pierce, who ministered in Brighton until 1923. He had been Rector of Wickford in Essex from 1899 till 1908, and, while there, published a book with the interesting title, "History of Wickford; Problems of a Pleasure Town." This might be a reference to the town gaining fame for being the place where naturism was born in the United Kingdom.

On 11th January 1908 the Church School at Wickford was destroyed by fire, but a new building was opened before it was time for Mr & Mrs Pierce to depart for Southend in the October of that year. He was vicar of St John's Southend until 1914 when he moved on to become Vicar of Prittlewell in Essex, the Rural Dean of Southend and an Honorary Canon of Chelmsford Cathedral.

He was instituted as Vicar of Brighton on 19th May 1917, but his time in Brighton was to be relatively brief. A temporary parish room had been in use since 1903,[1] but, after the end of the First World War, it was decided to build the Church Hall at St Peter's as a memorial to those who had been killed in the conflict. This project was very much masterminded by Pierce, but he never lived to see its completion, for he died on 2nd December 1923.

The local paper the following day ran the headline:

CANON DORMER PIERCE
Dies on his way to church at Brighton
Seizure in a Tramcar

The article continued:

"The Vicar of Brighton (the Rev Canon Dormer Pierce died with tragic sadness yesterday while he was on his way to the morning service at St Peter's Parish Church. He left Vicarage Lodge, Dyke Road, ... and walked to Seven Dials to take the Dyke Road Car down to the church. The tram reached the stopping place before the vicar got there and he is said to have run the last few yards to catch it. "Just a second please," he said as he reached it. He got in and took a seat in a corner.

Just as the car was reaching Preston Circus one of the other passengers drew Mr Hemen's (the conductor) attention to him saying he was in a fit. The vicar was still sitting in his corner, but a change had come over him and he appeared to have lost consciousness .... A moment later the vicar drew his last breath. The car was brought round to Preston Circus Police Station and the body was carried in."[2]

The cause of death was understood to be heart failure, but the circumstances of his passing must have been a tremendous shock to the parish. Thus when the Church Hall was completed in 1927, the windows on the south wall included an inscription which reads:

"In grateful memory of Francis Dormer
Pierce, Vicar of Brighton,
1917-1923 in whose heart it was to build
this hall."

Pierce is also remembered in the main body of the church where a bronze that dedicated the reredos in his memory still remains. He was buried at St Peter's, West Blatchington, where his grave is marked by a sizeable cross in the churchyard. This church had been restored towards the end of the nineteenth century and was reopened in 1891. As we have seen, it was in the care of the Vicars of Brighton, which explains why Pierce came to be buried there.

Dr Frederick Hicks succeeded Pierce as Vicar of Brighton in 1924. He was an ex-Territorial Army Officer, but also a scholar who was an authority on the training of men for the ministry. He was born in 1872 and was educated at Harrow and Balliol College, Oxford. After his ordination in 1897, he was based at Keeble College Oxford where he became Dean, before moving on to take up his appointment as Principal of Bishops' College, Cheshunt, where a future successor as Vicar of Brighton—Geoffrey Warde—trained under him.

He, thus, had held just one living—at Toddington in Bedfordshire—prior to coming to Brighton, but, according to the Brighton and Hove Herald, he proved himself to be an able parish priest, a splendid citizen and leader. Warde, who was the incumbent at St Peter's when Hicks died, spoke of him as a great spiritual teacher and leader, and felt he owed him a tremendous debt of gratitude for he had also served under Hicks as Dean of Gibraltar and later as Vicar of Grantham.[3]

Dr Hicks was consecrated as Bishop of Gibraltar in 1927 at Westminster Abbey. His first act as a bishop was to dedicate the Memorial Hall that was built adjoining St Peter's Church in memory of those who had been killed in the First World War. It was paid for out of donations that had been collected between 1921 and 1927. It features a stained glass window on its south wall that includes images of St Peter and St Wilfred[4], along with the inscription in Pierce's memory.

As Bishop of Gibraltar he had an extremely wide brief as he was responsible for churches all over mainland Europe. He was then appointed Bishop of Lincoln in 1932, and he held this position until his death on 10th February 1942. There is no doubt that the Brighton Vicarage housed some pretty distinguished clergymen of the Church of England during the twentieth century, for his obituary states:

"Canon Hicks was marked out for the highest office in the church even before he came to Brighton. His speeches in Convocation had been listened to with unusual attention . . . . He was known in Brighton and Sussex as a remarkably able preacher."[5]

Another future bishop, Alfred Rose, took over from Hicks as Vicar of Brighton and held the position from 1927 to 1935. He was born in 1884, and had been educated at Marlborough and Worcester College, Oxford. Before coming to Brighton he had been Vicar of Haigh in Greater Manchester, and prior to that, had served as a naval chaplain during the First World War. He was consecrated as Bishop of Dover in 1935, and remained there until his retirement in 1957, when he continued to serve as an Assistant Bishop within the Diocese of Canterbury and also as a Sub-Prelate of The Order of St John of Jerusalem. He died on 9th April 1971.

The reredos behind the High Altar was designed by W.H Randall Blacking in Flemish style during this time. It featured groups of figures—from left to right: The birth of Christ, the Wise Men at Bethlehem, the Crucifixion, the Supper at Emmaus and the Conversion of St Paul. In between them were the four evangelists and six saints. Above them was the figure of Christ in a canopy and on either side were St Peter and the Blessed Virgin Mary. It was completed in 1930, but it was unfortunately destroyed by fire in 1985.[6]

John How succeeded Rose as Vicar of Brighton in 1935. He was born in 1881 and ordained in 1906, after his education at Pocklington School and St John's College, Cambridge. He was Rural Dean of Liverpool before taking up his position at St Peter's where he was vicar until 1938, when he became Bishop of Glasgow and Galloway. During his time in Brighton, John Long was the organist and choirmaster up until 1938. His son, Canon Michael Long of St Andrew's Trowse Newton, writes affectionately of his boyhood memories of St Peter's in the thirties.

"I was very young and only six years old when we left Brighton.[7] My father had been appointed by Canon Rose, who, incidentally, I met in London when I was a student at King's College.

The vicar for most of our time was Canon How. I saw him from time to time over the years as he was educated at the same school in Yorkshire to which I went. I remember his two children, Martin and Ruth. My father held Canon How in high regard, as he was keen and supportive of the music.

The worship was well-ordered and I owe my earliest impressions of Church particularly to the Choral Eucharist on the first Sunday of each month. The dignity of the service, the colour of the vestments, the beauty of the music, sank deep down into my consciousness and here the seeds of my vocation were sown. On other Sundays the main morning service was Matins. The choir

was of a very high standard and there was a
wide range of anthems and settings."[8]

The addition of the chancel had certainly enabled St
Peter's to flourish musically during this century. While
vicar of Brighton, How was offered—but declined—the
Archbishopric of Brisbane in Australia. However, in 1946,
he went to less warmer climes when he was elected as
Primus of Scotland, which is the title of the presiding
bishop in the Church of the Scottish Episcopal Church.
He retired in 1952 and died on 22nd May 1961 in Hove,
with his funeral taking place at the Church of the Good
Shepherd on Dyke Road.[9]

We have already mentioned Geoffrey Warde, whose
dates as Vicar of Brighton coincided with the Second
World War. He was born in 1889 and was educated at
Tonbridge and Keble College, Oxford. He had been
Priest in Charge at All Saints, Pimlico, and then Vicar of
St Mark's Regent's Park, before serving under Dr Hicks as
Dean of Gibraltar and then as Rural Dean of Grantham.
After his time at St Peter's, he was archdeacon of
Carlisle, but returned to Sussex to become Bishop of
Lewes in 1946, and served there until his retirement in
1959. He died on 20th May 1972.

His successor as Vicar of Brighton was Frederick
Robathan, who was born in Gorakhpur, India, in 1896. He
was educated at King's School, Chester and Dean Close,
Cheltenham, before moving on to Oxford for his further
education at St Edmund Hall and Wycliffe Hall. He had
his early career experience in London where he was a
Minor Canon at firstly St Paul's Cathedral from 1928 to

1933 and then Westminster Abbey from 1934 to 1937. He then became Vicar of St John's Hackney, but also served as Chaplain to the Forces, before coming to Brighton in 1945.

It was during his time at St Peter's that the church was listed as a Grade Two building. This happened on 24th March 1951, and was going to have important implications for the future. It is interesting to surmise why St Peter's did not receive Grade One listed status. There are five churches in the city that are Grade One buildings. These are St Andrew's Church, Hove, which still has part of the original medieval structure, All Saints Church, the parish church of Hove, St Bartholomew's Church, Brighton, the "Noah's Ark Church" that dominates the area north of St Peter's, St Michael and All Angels Church, Brighton, a splendid example of a gothic revival church, and St Wulfran's Church, Ovingdean, the oldest church in the city.

Other notable buildings in the city that have achieved Grade One listed status include the Royal Pavilion, The Corn Exchange and Dome Theatre, Marlborough House, the West Pier and Stanmer House. Why St Peter's did not merit inclusion was perhaps due to the addition of the chancel which left the building with two distinct sections that rather struggled for compatibility. Despite this, Seldon places St Peter's at number six in his top ten of Best Brighton Buildings, behind the West Pier, the Royal Pavilion, Lewes Crescent, Brunswick Square and Brighton Railway Station, but in front of the Hippodrome, the Grand Hotel, Brighton College and Montpelier Villas.[10]

In 1953 Robathan moved on to become Canon of Ely where he was based until 1959. He became Vicar of Cardington in Bedfordshire in 1956 before taking up the position of Rector of Charleton near Kingsbridge in Devon in 1962 which he held until 1966. He died on 26th December 1986.

David Booth was the next Vicar of Brighton. He was born in 1907 and educated at Bedford School and Pembroke College Cambridge. He served as chaplain at Tonbridge School from 1935 to 1940 before acting as Chaplain to the Royal Naval Volunteer Reserve during the war. He became Rector of Stepney in 1945, before coming to Brighton in 1953. He was also the national chaplain to the Sea Cadet Corps.

During his time as Vicar of Brighton he sat on the town education committee, and was also one of the leading figures in the fight against the threatened closure of the Tarner Home.[11] In 1959, he left St Peter's to become Archdeacon of Lewes, and then, in 1972, he was appointed Headmaster of Shoreham College. During this time, he was also a Canon and Prebendary at Chichester Cathedral, until his retirement in 1977. He died on 24th March 1993.

Len Liechti lived in Brighton from 1949-1968, and is currently Assistant Practitioner at Royal United Hospital Bath. His memories of St Peters give an interesting "child's-eye view" of Sundays at St Peter's in the late fifties and early sixties:

"When I was nine (I was enrolled) in St Peter's Sunday School. For a year I stuck this out manfully, despite being the oldest pupil there by some margin and not exactly endearing myself by doe-eyed devotion to the elderly spinster ladies who ran the classes. (I did however enjoy the annual Sunday School outing to Bognor Regis, on a hired Southdown bus, with the highlight being a turn on the motor boats on the lake in Hotham Park.)

Perhaps recognising that I was a bit senior for Sunday School, the then vicar of St Peter's, invited me to become a Server. Eager to escape the elderly spinster ladies, and seeing the advantage of getting my compulsory weekly dose of religion over before lunchtime, I ended up wearing the full rig of cassock, smock and ruffled collar and carrying a candle on a pole behind the vicar as he processed up the aisle at communion. I recall sitting to one side of him opposite the choir as the prayers and hymns proceeded"[12]

By then John Keeling had succeeded Booth as Vicar of Brighton in 1960. He was born in 1907, and had begun as Vicar of St Thomas Newhey in 1935 where his ministry is described as "shot through with youthful enthusiasm." In 1937 he became an RAF Chaplain and had a long stint with the service until coming to St Peter's, where he was vicar until 1974.

The decoration of the ceiling of the chancel took place between 1967 and 1969. It begins over the altar with a description of creation, flanked by the crossed keys— the symbol of St Peter. Then come the bread and wine of the communion service, depicted by ears of wheat and a bunch of grapes. Following this, in the centre is Jesus Christ as the Light of the World (Lux Mundi), with symbols of the Trinity—the sign of the fish with the word, Trinitas, and the ship of the world (Navis Mundi), on either side.

As we move down the chancel we come to the Holy Spirit, seen in the form of a Dove, with the Latin for "Come Holy Spirit" (Veni Spiritus Sancte) running round the outside. The next two on the outside are a pelican—the sign of compassion (with the Latin for mercy, Misericordia) and a peacock—the sign of eternity (Aeternitas in Latin).

Then in the middle there is the Christian motif NIKA—a Greek word for victorious that symbolises Christ's conquest of death, and it is followed by an Anchor—the sign of hope (Spes Mundi)—and the initials INRI (Jesus of Nazareth King of the Jews) with the symbols of Christ's passion—the crown of thorns, the nails and the sword— above it. Finally the Greek letters Alpha and Omega—the Beginning and the End—complete this impressive work.[13]

John Hester was the next incumbent, spending spent ten years as Vicar of Brighton before going on to be a canon residentiary of Chichester Cathedral from 1985 to 1997. He was born at West Hartlepool in 1927 and was a student at St Edmund Hall in Oxford and Cuddesdon

Theological College. He was a curate at St George's church, Southall, in West London, from 1952 to 1955 and then spent three years as a curate at the church of the Holy Redeemer in Clerkenwell, where the possibility of a special ministry in the entertainment world was first recognised.

Thus in 1958 he was appointed as full-time secretary and organiser of the Actors' Church Union, with the responsibility of meeting the spiritual needs of the profession in theatres throughout the country. He ministered particularly to the acting profession as Rector of Soho from 1963 to 1975 for by then he was now senior chaplain of the Actors' Church Union. This was continued in Brighton among the seaside entertainers and he also took on the chaplaincy of Brighton and Hove Albion Football Club, which he held until his retirement from Chichester in 1997.

As Vicar of Brighton from 1975 to 1985, he had responsibility for many struggling parishes, and was also charged with appointment of clergy. Some like St John's and St Nicholas were united with Chapel Royal, but with further reorganisation needed he was appointed rural dean not only of Brighton but also of Kemp Town and Preston. In fact the parish of St Peter's was legally united with the Chapel Royal from 25th July 1978.

Meanwhile Hester was also fully involved in the civic life of the town. There were many civic services held at the church and a special occasion was on 5th June 1977, when there was a day of thanksgiving for the Silver Jubilee of H.M. the Queen's Accession. When Hester left St

Peter's in 1985 and moved to Chichester, his links with the theatrical world continued and he was able to become a trustee of the Festival Theatre. However it was it is said that what pleased him the most was receiving life membership of Equity. He died on 13th February 2008.

Dominic Walker became Vicar of Brighton in 1985. He was born in 1948 and was educated at Plymouth College and King's College, London. He was chaplain to the Bishop of Southwark after becoming a deacon in 1972. He went on to become Rector of St Mary's, Newington from 1976 to 1985, and is a life professed member of the Oratory of the Good Shepherd, an Anglican Religious Community and serving as its Superior from 1990-6.

In 1985, he was appointed Team Rector, Vicar and Rural Dean of Brighton and a Canon & Prebendary of Chichester Cathedral. He recalls that when he was appointed he was warned that the church building was not in great condition and that it had been built 'on the cheap' to provide a large parish church for the growing town of Brighton. Soon it became evident that a major restoration would be needed to be carried out and a professional fund raiser was employed.

His efforts were restricted by the fact that St Peter's is not listed as Grade One, for this limited access to grants. As a result there were difficulties in raising enough funds and the appeal was not a great success. However they were able to replace the roof over the organ, which was seen as a priority, and carry out some other emergency repairs. Although the congregation was growing at this time, they struggled to pay for the day-to-day running costs of the church so they were unable to contribute greatly to a restoration fund requiring millions.

The saddest event of this time was the destruction of the beautifully carved reredos in an arson attack on 4th September 1985.[14] The perpetrators of this act of vandalism put rags soaked in fuel behind the wooden figures before setting fire to it, but, prior to doing this, they also endangered themselves as the Argus reported:

> "Fire vandals who broke into St Peter's Church risked being crushed by the church's giant bells it was revealed today.
>
> The vandals smashed an inner door and then climbed a narrow spiral staircase to get into the belfry after breaking into the church in the early hours of yesterday.
>
> After climbing through the belfry (under the massive bells) the wreckers went on to the church roof and tried to force open a vent.
>
> Later they started a fire which caused more than £10,000 damage to the altar screen at the church in York Place. Many valuable carved wooden figures, including the altar centre piece—a figure of the Risen Christ— were badly damaged"[15]

There was an insurance claim, and this gave an opportunity to re-order the front of the church. The Diocesan Advisory Committee gave their advice on this rearrangement and suggested that the stone floor around the altar should be raised.

Meanwhile, Dominic Walker described how the focal point of the church was restored:

> "We commissioned John Armstrong to paint a crucifix for the high altar and gave him instructions to portray Jesus the Priest, but for the Christ figure not to look like a white Anglican cleric! So the figure portrays Jesus with brown skin and in a simple white robe with the cross keys and inverted cross of St Peter below."

Dr Eric Kemp was Bishop of Chichester from 1974-2001. He was one of the leading Anglo-Catholics of his generation and was keen that St Peter's should be a kind of cathedral for Brighton with a musical and preaching tradition. So by the 1980's there were thirty men and boys in the choir, a Director of Music, Assistant organist and organ scholar. As a result of the liturgical re-ordering after the fire, Bishop Eric used St Peter's for some diocesan events including the Chrism Eucharist during Holy Week when the bishop consecrated the holy oils and all the priests of the diocese came to renew their ordination vows.

St Peter's continued to be used for some civic and other big services, but many worshipped at St Peter's because they liked English choral music, appreciated the preaching or thought the other churches in Brighton were too high or too low. Dominic Walker, continuing with his recollections, referred to those living in the vicinity of the church:

"When I arrived, Brighton was seriously hit by many people with HIV/AIDS and I remember one young curate telling me after he had been there for over a year that he had not yet officiated at a funeral of someone older than himself. We had a number of large funerals for those who had died of AIDS.

Also during my time the 'spike' (homeless shelter) closed and the churches in Brighton got together to provide a night shelter staffed by volunteers. Churches Together also established a bereavement service and a number of the congregation trained as volunteers.

St Peter's was in a team with the Chapel Royal and St Nicholas so St Peter's people were able to use the facilities at the Chapel Royal to raise funds for local charities through a Saturday coffee shop and we had a parish lunch once a month in St Peter's Hall that was appreciated particularly by the older folk and those living alone.

We did manage to increase the congregation and also employed a full-time verger so that the church could be kept open during the day for those who wanted to come inside and look around or pray."[16]

Dominic Walker left Brighton to become Bishop of Reading in 1997, and then was appointed Bishop of Monmouth in 2003 when Rowan Williams moved from there to become Archbishop of Canterbury. He served there for ten years before retiring in 2013, and, as we have seen, speaks with affection of his time at the helm of St Peter's, while admitting that he was always aware that eventually there were going to have to be some hard decisions made about the viability of the building.

With many future bishops among the incumbents at St Peter's there was an obvious quality in leadership during the twentieth century. Therefore the question that needs to be asked at this point is why, despite such outstanding vicars during this time, did the church suffer such a decline in attendance that, a hundred years after the dedication of the chancel in 1906, was one of the factors that led to the looming threat of closure?

Changing patterns of church attendance undoubtedly had much to do with this. When St Peter's had been built, the influence of Wesley was still strong and the congregation numbers were of an order that encouraged the building programme that Henry Wagner and others had embarked upon. However, by the late Victorian era, music halls, sports clubs and newspapers were thought to contribute to the process of weaning people away from the churches.

There were other factors in this decline of church attendance. The church took a big knock from Darwinism which seemed to attack the Biblical basis of creation. Its response to the Scientists can be compared to the response that the Renaissance Church gave to those who claimed that the Earth went round the Sun. In both cases the church was seen as backward looking, and in an environment in which much wider educational opportunities enabled people to develop their own views on the issues of the time the teaching of the church often came into question.

Then there were the two World Wars in the first half of the Twentieth Century which shattered the confidence of a society that had entered that century in buoyant form. As Monica Furlong, referring specifically to the First World War, says,

> "The damage to religious faith came .... from the utter horror and disillusion of war itself, from the millions of young men . . . . who were killed .... not to mention the thousands who returned home with terrible wounds to bodies and minds. How could people reconcile a God of love with such evil, so many sufferings, so much hopelessness."[17]

These two major conflicts affected people in different ways. Some sought the comfort of the Church; others reacted strongly against it. As the values of the Church came under further discussion, there was a marked growth in the popularity of humanism as an alternative to Christian doctrine. Also, as this century wore on, there was even more leisure time than before, and people began to find alternative ways of spending their Sundays, with family outings becoming more attractive than anything the Church had to offer.

There was also disquiet concerning the Church's attitudes to sex. In the second half of the Twentieth Century, a much more liberal attitude to issues such as homosexuality, abortion and childbirth outside marriage was emerging. These were among the changing trends that society embraced during the decade that is often referred to as the "Swinging Sixties". The revolutions in music and fashion set the scene at this time as new ideas abounded and the spirit of the age was very much one of seeking personal freedom and satisfaction. Ten years on came a more ominous threat to the standpoint of the Christian message as the eighties embraced a "Loadsamoney" culture in which the acquisition of as much money as possible made it very much a decade of the worship of mammon.

How did these trends affect the levels of congregations at this time? Well between 1960 and 1985 the Church of England lost more than a third of its active membership. National church attendance in 1980 stood at 11% of the population; by 2005 it had fallen to 6.8%. St Peter's was not immune to this decline in congregational numbers. St Peter's average Sunday numbers had been 151 in the fifties, 138 in the sixties and 132 in the seventies, but this had dropped to 110 during the eighties. The first decade of the new century saw this average fall from 104 in 2000 to 75 in 2005 and 45 in 2008.[18]

The position of St Peter's as a "going concern" was particularly difficult because of the crippling expense of maintaining its building. For example, according to the log book of the church, in the period between 1994 and 2005, a total of £216,000.00 needed to be expended.

This included £18,000 for repairs to the organ chamber roof in 1994, £67,000 for nave roof repairs in 1996, £35,000 for clearance of asbestos from the undercroft in 1999, and £58,000 for replacement of roof gullies following dry rot in 2002-03—the latter which well-nigh bankrupted the church.[19]

With these expenses—that were over and above the costs of the everyday running of the church—it is no surprise that there was considerable doubt about the future of St Peter's during the early years of the twenty-first century. The church building is a massive structure, and there is an enormous amount of stonework that from the very outset needed to be looked after. The addition of the chancel and the hall obviously served to make this task even larger, but there were a number of factors that made it particularly vulnerable and difficult to maintain. Most of these are due to the location of the church, with its vicinity to the sea, and the years of weathering that would therefore be expected

Moreover there was also the threat that pigeons posed. Such a tall building was fully accessible to these birds, but over time they managed to block pipes, outlets and channels with their droppings. These droppings also had a harmful effect on the stonework with the acid, phosphates and nitrate salts they contained. The birds also caused erosion by pecking and alighting on the ledges around the roof.[20]

In the first century of the Church's existence, there was atmospheric pollution to the stonework which blackened the building. This was caused by the soot from domestic coal fires. Then there was the constant threat of contamination by wind-born sea salts, for being so close to the coast this was always going to be a problem. The ornate decorative cornices and parapets, together with other examples of carved stone were all affected by weathering, and there was a constant need to keep a close eye on the roof due to concerns over public safety.

If all this was not enough, it was stated in the Quinquennial Report of 1981 that the original Portland Stone of the building did not mix well with the Sussex Sandstone that was used to build the chancel extension. The calcium sulphate that results from the decomposition of Portland Stone can find its way into the sandstone and incur damage. No wonder, as the twentieth century went on the expenses associated with the church building began to mount.

Dominic Walker also recalled that the architect, who surveyed the state of the building during the 1980's questioned the removal of the galleries as he considered that they were integral in supporting the building. The galleries in the original Barry structure were taken down when the chancel was added, as were so many, as a result of the cultural and liturgical changes made in the wake of the Oxford Movement.

However the church did survive the "Great October Gale" of 1987, in which hurricane force winds came up the valley from the sea, ripping up trees as it approached St Peter's and then going on to flatten the elm trees on the Level to the north of the church. The result was that, with the absence of trees that had surrounded it, the building, once again, emerged into view, and could be seen much more clearly than before. Perhaps this return to public recognition was a portentous sign, as the next twenty years would see much debate about the future of the church.

6. The Threat of Closure

Douglas McKittrick became Vicar of Brighton in 1997 and Rural Dean of Brighton in 1998. He was born in 1953 and educated at John Marley School in Newcastle and St Stephen's House, Oxford. He was team vicar of St Luke in the City in Liverpool from 1981 to 1989 before moving on in the same city to be Vicar of Toxteth Park from 1989 to 1997.

He recalls being immediately impressed by the building and its choral tradition. What surprised him, though, was the eclectic nature of the congregation, with people coming from all over Sussex to worship. The magnificence of the music was one attraction, while another was that the style of worship was more moderate than the Anglo-Catholic tradition of other churches. In a sense it was more of a cathedral than a parish church.

One aspect that concerned him, though, was that the church was not very connected with the vibrancy and dynamism of Brighton, which was on the verge of receiving city status. The state of the building, of course, was also still a problem and in 1999, it was decided to launch another appeal. The Prince of Wales was invited to visit, and showed much interest in the church, expressing his support for the project.

On New Year's Eve that year there was a special service to celebrate the millennium which was jointly led by Bishop Eric Kemp and Cormac Murphy-O'Connor, the then Roman Catholic Bishop of Arundel and Brighton. The church was completely packed for the occasion, and after the service had finished it was decided to keep the church open. There had been a massive party in the Old Steine Gardens (one of the largest in the country) to usher in the new millennium, and now thousands of revellers were all going past the church as they made their way home.

Many hundreds poured into St Peter's, from midnight all the way through to four o'clock in the morning, when the church officials eventually decided that it really was time for bed! Reflection took many forms: standing, sitting, kneeling, lighting a candle; but somehow it seemed appropriate to pause and acknowledge this most momentous occasion in such a sacred place. According to Douglas McKittrick, "You could have heard a pin drop."[1]

Another memorable occasion at St Peter's took place the following year when Brighton and Hove Albion Football Club celebrated its centenary in 2001. A service of celebration took place at St Peter's, in which the church was full to capacity, with many in the congregation sporting the blue and white colours of the "Seagulls". It was a great occasion with all the players being present, along with the new Bishop of Chichester, John Hind. Interestingly, after going through the most turbulent times in their History during the nineties, the fortunes of the club dramatically changed with back to back promotions in the following two seasons.

In 2002 Douglas McKittrick was appointed Archdeacon of Chichester, a position he still holds at the time of writing. He was not replaced as Vicar of Brighton in 2002, and St Peter's was put in the care of David Biggs, who was appointed priest-in-charge. He had been vicar at the Chapel Royal since 1999, but some years before, in 1978, as we have seen, the two parishes had been linked together in an earlier deanery re-arrangement.[2] The responsibility for St Peter's was initially only going to be for a year, but eventually it was to last for eight. They were going to be extremely difficult years, with the very existence of the church being the subject of much debate.[3]

With mounting expenses and a deteriorating edifice to deal with, David Biggs had certainly taken on a massive additional burden. He recalls it was problems with the aisle roof on the London Road side—as we have seen from the log book—that really threatened the stability of the church finances. There now was a very real danger that St Peter's would share the same fate of some of the other nineteenth century churches in the city that that had been made redundant. However the first time that the future of St Peter's was called into question was in 2003, when the Brighton and Hove Deaneries Pastoral Strategy Review Group published its initial report. It stated that it cost £2 million to provide stipendiary clergy for Brighton and Hove while running costs amounted to £1 million.

Archdeacon McKittrick was Vice-Chairman of this group and was quoted in the Argus as saying, ""It is a terrible pity and breaks my heart, but the reality is we cannot expect the diocese to keep on pouring in hundreds of thousands of pounds of grants. We have tried to be very sensitive and will continue to listen to people but there has to be an air of realism." Concerning St Peter's, he added, "St Peter's needs at least to raise £2 million and it is not a growing congregation. The people who attend are faithful and fantastically musical but that does not sustain the building."[4]

One solution for the survival of St Peter's that was proposed by this report was to move the congregation of St Luke's Prestonville into the building. This would have seen the traditional form of worship of St Peter's replaced by a more modern style. This was disappointing to the current members of St Peter's but if the resources of St Luke's could make it viable, they would be happy to see their church survive. There was talk of clustering a number of parishes together and some radical thinking was encouraged by the Bishop.

St Luke's was a relatively strong position, as its congregation had grown from about 40 to around 250 over the previous four years, and there was also the possibility of its vicar, Peter Irwin-Clark, taking over the responsibility for the nearby St Bartholomew's as well. This idea produced some concern as the difference in churchmanship between these two congregations was fairly wide. Moreover the folk at St Luke's were not entirely sure about taking on the St Peter's building which needed so much money spending on it. The involvement of St Luke's was eventually ended when Peter Irwin-Clark decided to accept the position of Warham Missioner and Winchester Archdeaconry Faith Development Officer, and moved away from Brighton.[5]

Thus any envisaged link with St Luke's did not take place, and in April 2005 the Review Group's second report, which was entitled "Towards Revitalisation of the Church of England Deaneries of Brighton and Hove—the Next Steps," brought the news that St Peter's should close. This decision produced much reaction. Selma Montford, the secretary of The Brighton Society conservation group, reacting to the report said: "By far the most important building is St Peter's Church. It is very important to the landscape of the city." The Brighton Argus, in reporting the news said, "The Church of England hopes St Peter's can be kept open as a community centre, but conservationists are worried that would not generate enough income to maintain the building and could end up abandoned and decaying like Brighton's West Pier."[6]

However it was uncertainty that the congregation at St Peter's was left with. Over the next few years they remained hopeful as plans were laid to encourage new members, expand its services to the elderly and increase income by encouraging the church's use as a concert venue, as well as developing the church as an educational centre for local primary schools. But the edifice continued to deteriorate and when plaster began to fall from the ceiling at the back of the church, the diocese declared that the main body of the building was unsafe.

As a result the aisles and nave were taped off and services were confined to the area in front of the altar and the side chapel, with entry via the side door in Richmond Terrace. The reaction of the congregation varied from resignation to the inevitable closure on one hand to extreme fury that the church authorities were not doing more to save the historical building from further decay. At this point the Parochial Church Council (PCC) agreed to hold a special meeting on 6th October 2007 in order to vote on the issue of redundancy.

Half of the PCC were representatives of St Peter's while the other half were from the Chapel Royal. The Chapel Royal members had decided that they would not vote in favour of closure if their St Peter's counterparts were against it. However all bar one of the St Peter's members were in favour of closure. They had had first-hand experience of the difficulties that the church was in and by this stage were unwilling to continue supporting the church with their own finances, so they could see no other solution than to close the church.

Therefore, when the vote was carried in favour of redundancy at this meeting, this news led to great consternation among the congregation. Earlier in the year, they had had a meeting to discuss the proposed closure and had voted overwhelmingly against closure with only three out of the eighty in attendance being in favour. That had been in February 2007, and the following month they had formed a body called "The Friends of St Peter's Church". The formal objects of this group were agreed to be:

1. To safeguard and preserve St Peter's Church, the Parish Church of Brighton, as an historic and centrally important place of Christian worship.
2. To support the Church Committee, in liaison with the Parish Council, in maintaining the

services, fabric, fittings, ornaments, furniture and monuments of the Church and any land or buildings attached thereto, enhancing their beauty, safety and usefulness.

3. To encourage interest in and support for St Peter's Church in the local community, the Diocese and beyond.

4. To work with the Church Committee to develop and publicise the Church's mission to the city's residents and visitors and those who seek sanctuary, safety or refuge within the city.

On 26th May 2007 the steering Committee of the Friends of St Peter's Church agreed the following objectives:

1. To retain St Peter's as a working church.
2. To adapt the church building and hall for multiple community use, including secular activities.
3. To maximise income in order to safeguard the church's work.
4. To appoint a permanent priest.

In June a petition with nearly 4,000 signatures that protested against plans to close St Peter's was handed to the Revd. Ian Gibson, the chaplain for the Bishop of Chichester. This particular campaign had been launched by a group of young people who had spent the previous two months campaigning at the Brighton Open market every Saturday morning.[7] It had also been endorsed by BBC presenter, Jeremy Paxman, whose career had started with Radio Brighton in the early seventies.

But, as was feared, the Bishop of Chichester endorsed the recommendation that St Peter's should be made redundant because of dwindling congregations. The Argus reported in September 2007:

> "Church bosses have announced they want to close Brighton and Hove's 'cathedral'.
>
> The landmark St Peter's Church in York Place, Brighton, should close because of small congregations and high maintenance costs, according to the Diocesan Pastoral Committee.
>
> The recommendation from the committee, which is in charge of churches in the city, comes after seven months of consultations and meetings.
>
> A letter has been sent to the Church Commissioners, a Church of England body, who will make a final decision on the plans after a 28 day consultation. Campaigners believe this is the final chance to stop the church from closing. They are calling for everyone opposed to the closure plans to respond to the commissioners who will be asking all "interested parties" for their views. The Friends of St Peter's Church is also asking people join them in services and choir to strengthen the congregation.

Parishioners, wardens and residents were shocked when plans to make the landmark building "redundant" and send its congregation to other churches in the area were revealed in February. Fears were raised as to what would happen to the grade II listed building, which many see as a 'gateway to the city'.

But Steven Sleight, secretary of the Diocesan Pastoral Committee, said "there was absolutely no intention that the building would disappear from the cityscape". He said there was no way it would be demolished even though thousands of pounds had been paid out for emergency repair work on the "deteriorating building". Mr Sleight said the Diocese would be expected to find another use for the church if their recommendation was approved by the commissioners.

He said: "I am not going to speculate on what St Peter's could be used for—it could be any of a number of options. You have only to look in Brighton and Hove to see the variety of things it could become. St Patrick's is a night hostel, Holy Trinity in Duke's Street an art gallery and St Thomas is being used for another congregation. Parts of the fabric of St Peter's are falling apart but I do not think there is any chance of it being knocked down. Even if we wanted to we have got a cat in hell's chance of getting it approved—it is a listed building."

Maureen Dickson, the secretary of the Friends of St Peter's Church, said: "It is very important that people do not give up. Many, many, people in Brighton have said they do not wish to see St Peter's close. The Diocese has indicated that St Peter's is only one of many, many churches in Brighton, but we need to show the commissioners that it is very special, because it is considered to be Brighton's cathedral."[8]

There was a further report in the Argus in October 2007, confirming the decision of the PCC to support the redundancy of the church

"The church known as Brighton's cathedral appears doomed to closure. An influential committee voted on Sunday to recommend that the landmark St Peter's Church in York Place be made redundant. The margin of the vote was reported to be overwhelming. Despite being the city's biggest and best known church the Parochial Church Council responsible for it has decided that it is no longer viable to pay the maintenance bills to keep it running.

The recommendation from the PCC, whose members are drawn from the congregation of St Peter's and the nearby Chapel Royal in North Street, will now be passed to the Church of England's Church Commissioners to make a final decision. But it is believed that it will now be extremely difficult to overturn the recommendation.

The council's decision has come despite a surge of opposition towards the closure from residents of the city. More than 6,000 people have written letters or signed their name to petitions calling for it to be saved. Several vigils have been held and actress Dora Bryan has played her part, leading a "knit-in". Their efforts were well received by the church's own committee, which has expressed an opinion that it would be possible to keep it running with better organisation and more use of the building as a venue for concerts and other revenue sources. They were not enough to influence the council.

The national Church Commissioners will carry out an extensive consultation before reaching their conclusion, giving parishioners a final chance to try to keep St Peter's open. The closure was originally recommended by the Anglican Diocese of Chichester in light of dwindling congregation and repair bills of thousands of pounds which it said would not be viable. Recently plaster has fallen from the roof onto the floor of the Grade II listed building."[9]

In response to this, in November 2007, the Friends Group then urged supporters to write to the Church Commissioners who had begun a period of formal consultation over the proposed closure. As well as the letters of support, there was a Letter of Appeal which was sent to the Commissioners as a "mini petition" but signed only by those who attended St Peter's. It is worth recording the wording of the appeal as it provides a clear insight into the feelings and aspirations of the people involved.

> "We, the undersigned, are members of the congregation of St Peter's Church, the Parish Church of Brighton, and attend either at the morning service or at evensong. Some of us have been members of this parish family for many years and some for a shorter time.
>
> We are writing to express our disagreement with the Diocese of Chichester's proposal to close St Peter's. We hope that the Church Commissioners and national leadership of the Church of England may take a different view and help us retain the church for multiple use—both as a worship space and a venue adapted for independent community activities and ventures. We have always been open to shared use.
>
> We are prepared to work with the Diocese and outside agencies to safeguard and develop the building, provided that we can retain some part of the church for regular

worship and, ideally have occasional access to the main body of the building for large or religious community events.

Over the years that the church has been under threat the congregation has not wavered in its opposition to redundancy. In February 2007 the congregation of St Peter's met to discuss the proposed closure and decided overwhelmingly to retain St Peter's as a worship space. Only three of the eighty people who attended the meeting disagreed.

The City Council has passed a resolution supporting this view and well over 6,000 of the city's people have signed a petition in agreement.

We are aware that the church needs repair, but believe this is not an argument for closure. Representatives of English Heritage have advised us that they are more likely to fund repairs to a working church than a redundant one.

St Peter's Church is of enormous symbolic importance to this city because it is the most prominent and visible Christian church and because it is well known to be the Parish Church of Brighton, traditionally the site of civic ceremonies and other major events. The church also contains the city's war memorials. It is, as one local woman said "our St Paul's".

We hope and prayer that the Church of England will not allow this closure to go ahead. We call upon the national leadership of the Church of England, the Church Commissioners, English Heritage and our local Council to do all they can to save our church for the sake of the community it serves and the generations to come."

The Convenor of the Friends was Jean Calder, a former Brighton Borough Councillor and columnist for the Argus, whose article in the paper in September 2006[10] had highlighted the need to keep the church open in order to serve the local community. There were plenty of ideas, with one of the options she mentions in this article being plans that the council had for developing the area as a cultural centre. In the meantime the church authorities were hamstrung by lack of resources for St Peter's was not the only church in the city that was threatened with closure.

There were many concerns. It was feared that if St Peter's was closed the Diocese would find it much easier to close other churches in the city, particularly if they happened to be situated on prime building land. Closer to home the deteriorating state of the building was a constant worry. It was not going to get any better and if the church was closed the building would get even worse. Then there would be a fear of vandalism and demolition could then become a possibility. As one parishioner said, despairingly, "The city will have another West Pier on its hands, but one that is even more visible"

Brighton's West Pier had fallen into disrepair over the previous forty years, and was now a burnt out, skeletal wreck, marooned out of reach from the shore and giving a most melancholy reminder that it had indeed seen better days. There was a real fear that St Peter's could go the same way.

The Friends achieved good coverage in the local media and worked with the City Council, assisting the Leader's Office to draft a resolution aimed at saving the church. It achieved all-party support and this was followed by the Council accepting an invitation for the Mayor of Brighton and Hove to be appointed Patron of the Friends. They were certainly grateful to receive such support from local politicians.

7. Holy Trinity Brompton

As a result of all the local publicity that the Friends of St Peter's had received during 2007, there was much interest among the community of Brighton and Hove—which had gained City status as part of the millennium celebrations in 2000. A Hove resident, Pat Haith, passed on all that was going on to her son, Jamie, who was an ordained Anglican minister on the staff of Holy Trinity Brompton. [1]

Holy Trinity Brompton is a London church, about the same age as St Peter's, but which had fared much better than St Peter's during the last quarter of the twentieth century. It had become well known for pioneering the Alpha Course which had won worldwide appeal as a tool for introducing the basics of the Christian faith. It could very much be said to be at the forefront of church revival during the years that traverse the end of the twentieth century and the beginning of the twenty-first, attracting a younger generation of worshippers with a formidable zest for the Christian gospel.

Another facet of the work of HTB (as it is familiarly known) was the sending out of church planting teams to redundant churches in London. Over a twenty-five year period these plants had been averaging at about one a year, but all of them had been in the metropolitan area. Now Jamie Haith brought to his colleagues the possibility of a new plant outside London—in "London by the Sea" as Brighton is sometimes affectionately nicknamed. This resulted in the Vicar of HTB, Nicky Gumbel, writing to the Church Commissioners, expressing an interest in the possibility of sending a planting team to Brighton.

In April 2008 Nicky Gumbel met with the Bishop of Chichester, the Archdeacon and other diocesan officials to explore the matter further. It is understandable that the diocese were not too keen with this last minute proposal, for they had explored all the possibilities over the last five years and it seemed that the only conceivable outcome would be further delay to what had already been a difficult and heart-rending process. However John Hind, the Bishop, was won over and warmed to the possibility of HTB involvement.

Meanwhile the Church Commissioners met in May 2008 to discuss the proposed redundancy of St Peter's. A group of the Friends travelled up to London, and four of them were able to give verbal evidence to the commissioners. These were Jean Calder and her daughter Clare, Isabel Turner and Janet King. Other people, such as Barney Paine along with George and June Austen, came up with them to support the cause with banners, but most of the people in the campaign to save the church were quite elderly and couldn't travel.

Jean Calder describes these petitioners as being "a bit of a rag, tag and bobtail group," and, by all accounts the commissioners were not used to lay groups from congregations taking on their local priests and the church hierarchy in quite the way they did. Moreover the leadership among the Friends happened to be female and this further underlined the extraordinary nature of this meeting.[2]

The spirit and endurance of the Friends of St Peter's in rallying to the cause cannot but be admired, but, at the same time, there must also be sympathy for the diocesan authorities, who simply just did not have the resources to look after a building that, to coin a couple of modern phrases, had been "built on the cheap" and was decidedly "high maintenance". The figure of three million pounds was quoted as the sum needed to fully repair the building. Many believed that this was not the best use of church finances and found it difficult to justify such an expense.

There was also a hindrance to fundraising as the Friends became aware that potential donors were unwilling to become involving in raising substantial amounts of money unless there were guarantees that these funds would be used entirely on the church. The fear was that if the church was made redundant it would be sold off to developers, and there was a real reluctance to give money that "ultimately might benefit private business interests."[2] The Friends were also unable to apply for grant aid for restoration because they had no legal responsibility for the building.

The Annual Report of the Friends in 2008 also records that:

> "The Friends are very conscious that the church has a special place in the hearts of the people of the city and within the local

community. We are acutely aware that redundancy would have a devastating impact upon local residents and shop keepers, already demoralised by closures in the London Road shopping area.

St Peter's has for many years been a place in which elderly people, those low on incomes and others with mental health problems, addictions or other vulnerabilities can feel at home. We felt strongly that despite the fact that the church was under threat, we should actively develop and maintain this aspect of St Peter's work.

As a consequence, the Friends set up a small project which we called the St Peter's Community Project (SPCP). This had the great benefit of involving and drawing together people of no faith or different faith, in work that many Christians might term "mission", but which others would recognise as "community work".[3]

At this stage the main argument from the Friends was that there was a continued pastoral need for keeping the church open. However they were also able to point out that Holy Trinity Brompton had offered assistance. It was to the great relief of the Friends that the Commissioners refused to accept the Diocese's proposal for redundancy and asked the Bishop to explore other options, in particular the offer of help from HTB.

There was widespread relief and delight with the reaction to this decision being felt way beyond the boundaries of the city. Canon Michael Long, whose recollections have been mentioned earlier, wrote to Jean Calder in May 2008:

> "I am delighted to hear the encouraging news about St Peter's—a due reward for the truly immense and impressive work done by you and the Friends. Looking at the pastoral work that is being done from St Peter's, there can be no justification to say that it has no future role".[4]

There were then consultations between the diocese and HTB who had set up a charity called the "Church Renewal Trust". There were various legalities that needed working through, especially as they were dealing with building that needed a massive amount of money spent on it. What they came up with was a joint patronage between the Bishop of Chichester and the Vicar of Holy Trinity Brompton, so that The Church Renewal Trust took on ownership of the building on a 125 year lease from the diocese, while the Bishop was given the responsibility of choosing the vicar.

It was also decided that although St Peter's was to remain a parish church, its parish was in fact just to be the footprint of the church. Now that the union with the Chapel Royal was to be dissolved, it had the rest of the land as its parish—apart from St Peter's on its traffic island. These negotiations took the best part of a year and it was not until May 2009 that the parties involved went public with announcement that St Peter's had been saved. The Argus reported:

> "An iconic church has been saved after a plan to hand it over to a London-based Anglican group was approved. St Peter's Church in York Place, Brighton, faced closure after falling congregation numbers and structural disrepair made it financially unsound.
>
> But this week Holy Trinity Brompton, a world renowned Anglican group who first developed the Alpha Course, agreed to take over the running of the church. For more than a year it looked as though Grade II listed St Peter's—one of Brighton's most prominent landmarks—might be closed as a place of worship and converted into a cafe or shops.
>
> But under the new pastoral scheme approved by the Church Commissioners on Tuesday St Peter's will remain under Church of England control. It will be leased by the Chichester Diocesan Fund and Board of Finance to HTB who will maintain the building and run services. The parish and benefice of Brighton and St Peter with the Chapel Royal will be dissolved and two new parishes and benefices created—Brighton The Chapel Royal and Brighton St Peter.
>
> Jean Calder, convenor of the Friends of St Peter's Church said: "We welcome the help of

HTB. We accept the proposed division of the two parishes and note that although the new parish of St Peter will be reduced in size, this might make it easier for the church to serve the city as a whole."

But the group have made a request to the Church Commissioners that worship continue during the handover period. Ms Calder added: "After the epic struggle to save the church, the last thing the congregation needs is to be dispersed, which would create a risk of vandalism. It is vital to ensure the period of redundancy is for a matter of hours, rather than days, weeks or months."

But a spokesman for the Diocese of Chichester says this is unlikely. The Revd David Guest (Communications Officer for the Diocese) said: "This is just one early step in a long process—nothing is confirmed for sure. We must now partake in further legal discussions and also perhaps the repair of the church roof before Holy Trinity Brompton could arrive. The church may well have to close until the final details of the agreement are decided upon and dates are fixed by the bishop. It is a little bit like selling a house—you wouldn't expect to have people moving in the next day, there are a lot of legal details to be dealt with. Hopefully it will be no more than a matter of months and then we can all join hands and reopen St Peter's with HTB."

> A spokesman from HTB said: ""It has
> been a privilege to work with the diocese
> of Chichester on the future of St Peter's
> Brighton and we are grateful to the Bishop
> and his leadership team for all their
> encouragement and support. We are excited
> to have been invited to play a part in the
> diocese's vision for a new chapter in the life
> of St Peter's."[5]

In the event the last Sunday service was held at St
Peter's on 21st June 2009. Then there was a formal
service on 29th June 2009—St Peter's Day—that closed
the church prior to its reopening in November. Many
former parishioners were invited back for this occasion
and there were about seventy in the congregation that
day. Conditions in the church were far from ideal with
the nave in such a state of disrepair that it was roped off.
There had been no heating in the church for about five
years and Sunday services had had to be held in the Hall.
In effect, therefore, the church was closed for just four
months, although during this time the Friends' group still
maintained services, even holding some of them in the
local Fish and Chips shop.

Meanwhile at the HTB end, now that the project was
public knowledge, team building could begin in earnest.
Archie Coates, an ordained Anglican minister on the
HTB staff, had agreed to lead the team. His wife, Sam,
had grown up in Brighton, where she still had family,
so for her the move was going to be like coming home.
For others there was quite a bit of uprooting to do, but
gradually a group came together and by November it

was fifty strong. It included the HTB vicar's son, Jonny Gumbel, who was going to be the curate.

During this interim period before St Peter's could officially be reopened, Archie Coates was licensed as Priest in Charge—thus taking over from David Biggs. This enabled the new regime to have the keys of the church and begin to do some of the necessary work before services could safely be held there. It was at this point, on 1st July 2009, that the two churches became legally divided. Then on 29th October, Archie Coates was inducted as vicar in readiness for the reopening of the church on 1st November. The Argus reported the following day:

> "Holy Trinity Brompton's first church plant outside London was officially launched last night when the Bishop of Chichester, John Hind, inducted former HTB Associate Vicar Archie Coates as Vicar of St Peter's Brighton. More than 250 people, including the Vice Lord Lieutenant and the Mayor, packed the chancel of St Peter's for the ceremony.

> HTB director of classical music, Simon Dixon, played the organ and a choir from HTB sang at the event. A worship band was led by Paul Nelson, who has joined the Brighton team. The Rev'd Jonny Gumbel, who will be Archie's curate also took part in the service. The Bishop spoke of his gratitude towards HTB Vicar, Nicky Gumbel, for his role in saving St Peter's, which was on the verge of

redundancy. A team of more than 50 HTB members have joined Archie to make the plant possible."[6]

The church was re-consecrated as a place of worship as well as being re-licenced for weddings, etc. But when the first services were held on 1st November the only area that was safe for the congregation to be admitted to was in the chancel. Despite the obvious discomfort and the ominous look of the state of the inside of the church, this was just the start for those who had committed themselves to help restore St Peter's to its former glories. One report read as follows:

"As the first of the vintage cars wends its way into Brighton on 1 November and completes the Veteran Car Run that began in London earlier in the day, St Peter's Church in this seaside city will be embarking on a big adventure that also started in the capital. The journey began in earnest in 2008 when Holy Trinity Brompton—the home church of Alpha—expressed an interest in the Grade II listed building which had a dwindling congregation and was facing closure.

After more than 6,000 people signed a petition to keep this Brighton landmark open, and HTB asked the Church Commissioners if they could plant a church here, Rev Archie Coates's feet have barely touched the ground. "We've masses to do still, and we've hardly made a dent in it," said Archie who used to be HTB's associate vicar and was inducted as vicar of St Peter's by the Bishop of Chichester, Rt Rev John Hind on 29 October. "It needs £3million spending on it. We've no idea how we'll raise the money. It's quite an adventure."

"Around 50 grown-ups from HTB and their families have already relocated to the city, and in recent months have been wielding paintbrushes and cleaning equipment to make part of the building habitable. We can't meet in the main part of the church at the moment, but we've been given permission to move the choir stalls from the chancel and have space for about 250 people. We have screened off the rest of the church as it's currently unsafe."

Other churches in the city have been very positive about keeping the building open and to HTB moving in. "Anglican churches and others have said: 'the more the merrier.' One Anglican clergyman said he feared that St Peter's would become another West Pier and if it crumbled it would show that the Church is dead. Archie has no intention of letting this happen. Nor has the Bishop of Chichester who is fully behind the project.

And St Peter's is not letting the grass grow. The first of its five-week Alpha courses begins on Wednesday 11 November—and the congregation has already been exploring ways of getting involved in local social action. It hopes to be working with charities and other groups such as Off the Fence, Citylight, FairShare and the YMCA, as well as the local police.

"We want to be a blessing to this city by partnering with local charities who are helping vulnerable woman, the homeless and so on." As he starts out in this the first HTB church plant outside London, Archie said he is "really looking forward to it. "It's going to be quite an adventure, but great fun—and it's great to be in something right at the beginning."[7]

As Archie Coates prepared to reopen the church and begin services, he was very encouraged to see the amount of goodwill there was towards St Peter's. This made him realise why so many people had signed the petition to keep the church open as a place of worship. In those early weeks he had meetings with Council leaders, church leaders, Chief Superintendents, local businesses and charity CEOs, all initiated by them, to discuss how we might work together for the city. In particular, the police wanted to get together because "we're in the same business as you are—peace and justice."

8. Serving the People of the City

Sunday 1st November 2009 was a memorable day—the start of a new adventure. The church hall was packed when we arrived for the evening service, with the buzz of conversation and the serving of teas, coffees and cakes, amid an atmosphere of excitement and anticipation. Then it was time to go through to the church and when we entered we could see the nave area on our right looking eerie and desolate. It was also unsafe, owing to the risk of falling masonry, and so was blocked off.

We moved round into the chancel area and shortly the service began. Paul Nelson began with some songs of worship and then it was the turn of Archie Coates, together with his wife Sam, to enlarge the vision for the new project which is to play a part in the re-evangelisation of the nation and the transformation of society. A total of 600 people had squeezed into one of the three services on that re-opening day and the re-launch was under way.

Many people had come down from London to support the team on that first Sunday, but a week later there were still good numbers as local people returned and many others, including students, came for the first time,. That week an Alpha Course began in the Moksha Café over the road from the church, and there was an encouraging number at the first evening. The second Alpha in January 2010 took place in the church hall, and, as numbers continued to increase, by September 2010, it had moved into the church itself. Then in January 2011 a Morning Alpha was launched, while a Students' Alpha was introduced the following year, and in 2013 Alpha Courses were run specifically for the guests at Safehaven.

"Safehaven" came about in the following way, The aim of the church plant had always been to serve the local community, and "serving the people of the city" is an apt description of the years at St Peter's after the reopening. At first the team were not sure what form this service would take, but, just before the church was reopened, in September 2009, a young woman called Mel died of a heroin overdose on the steps of St Peter's.

A memorial service was held for her in the church; and it was now realised that their building was located in the middle of an area of the city that was frequented by the street community. In response to this need, Jonny and Tara Gumbel were charged with the running of the Helping People team, which was formed for the purpose of making a difference to the community and society in the neighbourhood.[1]

This resulted in the launch of the Safehaven project for the homeless, in February 2010. The name was well chosen, as St Peter's soon became known as a safe place where there was shelter from the storms of turbulence and hardship. There were twenty-five guests for the Saturday evening meal on that first occasion, but this number has steadily risen to a hundred which is as many as the catering facilities can cope with.

As numbers grew the location of the meal moved from the hall into the church. Besides the enjoyment of the meal, there is also the chance to find a sense of dignity, safety, and community. A short service was added on at the end of the evening to give the guests a chance to engage spiritually as well, and this proved to be a much appreciated development.

It was then felt that the church could do more than just the Saturday night, and wanted to build up relationships with the street people during the week. Sam Coates, with a particular vision of reaching out to ladies in distressing situations, gathered a team together to run "Safehaven Women" on a Thursday afternoon. This really was a "safe haven", for while there was a provision of food, drink, hair dressing, manicure and pedicures, facials, exercise, craft sessions and a clothing bank, there was also the opportunity to develop a warm, friendly atmosphere where guests would feel welcome and appreciated.

When the undercroft of the church was refurbished with the addition of new toilet facilities, there was also the addition of a shower which became another feature of the Safehaven work. When Safehaven Men was later introduced by Tom Bucher, in October 2012, on Friday afternoons, there was, once again, a steady growth in attendance. Besides the refreshments and clothing bank, there were art and music sessions, table-tennis and board games as well as a chance to peruse the newspapers.

A development to this work took place when the St Patrick's Nightshelter for the homeless—the only one in the city—was due to close on 31stJanuary 2012. In response to this St Peter's proposed the idea of sharing the nightshelter operation with six other churches—each doing one night a week. Amazingly, all of the churches involved got the day of the week they wanted, and preparations went ahead to open up this new project on 1st February (in thick snow) under the name of the Brighton and Hove Charities Nightshelter.

This was repeated during the winter of 2012-13, when the months of December to February were covered, although there was an extension into March that winter when temperatures were still low, with snow on the ground. In 2013-14, four months are due to be covered as it is planned to run from 23rd November—28th March. St Peter's co-ordinated the operation, registering the clientele and moving camp beds round the city between the sites each day in a van.

This project was not only serving the needs of the homeless in a really important way, but also saw churches working together. The other churches that were involved covered a variety of denominations and included. All Saints Church, Hove; Bishop Hannington Church, Hove; Church of Christ the King, Brighton; Sacred Heart Roman Catholic Church, Hove; St Andrews Church, Hove; St Joseph's Roman Catholic Church, Brighton; The Church on the Rock, Brighton; and The One Church, Brighton.

As we have seen, besides the regular Sunday services, the two main ways of serving the people of the city that were instituted in the early months since the reopening were Alpha and Safehaven. But, as time went on, a number of specialist courses were organised to meet specific needs. These are called Family Life courses and are mostly run by volunteers. All the courses emanate from Holy Trinity Brompton. Each course is started when a clear need and demand from people is identified, and when there is someone who is passionate about running it. They are open to anyone whether they go to St Peter's, to another church or to no church at all.

In October 2010 two practical courses were launched. One was the "Marriage Course" which had the aim of making good marriages better. The other, in contrast, was the "Divorce and Separation Course" which aimed to help people move on from the pain and reality of a break-up in a relationship. Both these courses are run twice a year. The Marriage Course is held in the church hall with approximately ten to eight couples attending each time. It is open to any married couple whether in the congregation or not. The Divorce and Separation Course usually has around six to ten people.

The "Recovery Course" is open to anyone struggling with any kind of addiction, whether it is to alcohol, drugs, pornography, over-eating or any other compulsive behaviour. It is a confidential, sixteen week, Christian programme, based on the Twelve Steps used by Alcoholics Anonymous and Narcotics Anonymous. The "Bereavement Course" started in March 2013, with ten people. As with the other courses, it is run on a regular basis. This course is for anyone who has experienced a significant bereavement, whether recently or many years ago, and feels they would benefit from spending time in a safe environment exploring some of the issues around the grieving process. It is open to all, whether from a background of any faith or none at all, and takes the perspective that those that are on the grief journey can learn from each other's experience along the way.

The "Marriage Preparation Course" was started in February 2011 and is both for couples who are getting married at St Peter's and for any other engaged couple who would like some marriage preparation, with around five or six couples attending each time. The "Parenting Children Course" started in February 2013. It was held in the church hall during the day, so was mainly attended by one parent from each family. It is linked to the Tots & Toddlers group which was established shortly after the opening of the church. This runs every Thursday morning in the Church Hall for pre-school children and their parents or carers, many of whom are not regular attenders at St Peter's.

The "Money Course" was launched in January 2012, after those running it had received training from an organisation called "Christians Against Poverty". Twenty people signed up for the first course and since then well over a hundred have attended it. Over three evenings it goes through practical ways of managing money better, and has resulted already in many people becoming much more positive in their attitude to money.

One feature of all these courses is that you don't have to attend the church services to go along to them. It is the same with Safehaven and Alpha, and the other similarity is that they all involve eating together as part of the evening. In the four years since the reopening of the church, many people in the city have been helped through these courses. The re-launched St Peter's can certainly be said to be "serving the people of the city".

Meanwhile there were building repairs to be seen to and, with a grant from English Heritage and the Heritage Lottery Fund of £199,000[2], this essential work began soon after the reopening. Teams of church members were able to help with some basic maintenance work to parts of the building that could be easily reached, but, up above, there were conservation repairs needed to the aisle roofs, nave roof structure, clerestory walls and plaster ceilings.

The report of the architect is worth quoting as it reveals the extent of the work that has been undertaken:

> "One of the challenges of this first phase of repairs at St Peter's is the fact that much of the work undertaken cannot be seen internally from the ground floor or from the outside. If you live on the upper sides of the valley either side of St Peter's, you might catch a glimpse of the new zinc roof to the side aisles, or inside you can see patches of plaster repair left undecorated, so as to spread the limited funds available, as far as possible.
>
> The fact is that much of the work is hidden away from the public and cannot be seen, yet it has been essential work to undertake, to enable a young, vibrant and growing

congregation reclaim this church from the threat of redundancy and breathe new life into the Christian mission and build community in the centre of Brighton."[3]

So the work that was completed was as follows:

1. Renewing the roof coverings of the side aisles and lower tower, with the addition of necessary ventilation as well as inspection hatches to facilitate future monitoring of the state of the structure.
2. Carrying out plaster and timber repairs to the nave and aisle ceilings.
3. Undertaking remedial repairs to the nave roof structure, where serious defects were discovered that had gone unnoticed for a fair period of time.
4. Re-pointing the clerestory walls, where joints in the masonry had been opened up, in order to maintain a watertight structure.
5. Repairing masonry where iron cramps had corroded and damaged the stone.

The architect's report constantly refers to budgetary constraints during the completion of the work. While all essential repairs were carried out, there will be much more to be done in the near future, and the work to restore the Tower will be another expensive project that the Church P.C.C. will need to plan for. Although the church was made secure inside for everyday use, some of the outside walls at the south end and round the tower have remained fenced off.

Inside the church there was also much activity as during the summer of 2012, new toilets and a shower were installed in the basement (or crypt) area. As well as this there was also some essential work undertaken to remove asbestos from parts of the building, while underfloor heating was installed in the church. This did not mean that that temporary heaters and blowers, that had been taking the chill off worshippers since the reopening, could be stood down straight away, as the boiler to fire up the new central heating system was not operational until September 2013.

During the course of all this necessary repair work, the nave and side aisles, that were part of Barry's original structure, were taken out of use, leaving only the chancel and side chapel—as well as the hall—available for the purposes of the church. With the church growing in number, as the Electoral Roll records, it became increasingly difficult to accommodate everyone comfortably, and there was very much a "pioneer spirit" in services at this time. In January 2012, just over two years after the re-opening, the east aisle was opened up and then in July that year the whole space became available as the two year repair project was finally completed.

The Church Electoral Roll recorded 181 members in April 2010; 255 members in April 2011; 298 members in April 2012 and 378 members in April 2013.[4] These figures give a sense of how the church developed numerically during this time, while not being an exact representation. For when the whole interior of the church was made available in July 2012, it was reported that six hundred people came to services that first Sunday after the scaffolding was taken down—although visitors coming for christenings did swell the number on that occasion.

Such a turnaround in the fortunes of St Peter's did not escape the local media, for on the same day that an article appeared about a cash crisis for Sussex Anglican churches, the Brighton Argus, under the headline of "Churches success in wake of Sussex C. of E. crisis", reported:

> "Three years ago, St Peter's Church in York Place, Brighton, was threatened with closure under the Diocese of Chichester's management. However, under the energetic leadership of Reverend Archie Coates the prominent church has become a thriving, active church attracting a large congregation of students and doing outstanding work for the city's homeless.
>
> Rev Coates said: "It's a question of community and building a relationship with the community. The hardest thing is to get people who have misconceptions or preconceptions about church across the front door, but when they come in and meet a welcoming and diverse ward those barriers begin to break. We have an Alpha Course, and currently 80 people attending, which is a practical introduction to Christianity for people who don't go to church. It's an easy forum for anyone to come in and discuss any

issues. We also run a recovery course for people who struggle with addiction. It's all about finding ways to be relevant to the local community."[5]

That summer the decision was taken to use Sir Charles Barry's original interior for the main services by turning the congregation round to face south. Archie Coates, while explaining that the change would accommodate the congregation much more comfortably as the use of the side aisles would give a greater width to the seating arrangements, jokingly added that those who were disappointed that they could no longer see the magnificent window at the north end of the church should be comforted that he himself now had a good view of it!

This move brought the congregation back into Barry's "open meeting-room"—as described by Burton and Sitwell. It makes one wonder what the great architect would think. After part of his original work had been demolished to make way for the building of the chancel, it was now to his part of the church that the focus of worship was returning. And as this happened, the magnificence of Barry's interior, now that it had been restored and fully carpeted, was much admired and appreciated by a new generation of worshippers.

Of course, Church of England traditions, concerning the direction congregations should worship, had been broken from the outset at St Peter's. Being built on a north/south axis meant that the adjective "liturgical" was used to describe the direction. Thus the chancel was built in the liturgical east—though, in common parlance, it faced north. Now, in September 2012, the niceties of direction were replaced by the practicalities of managing a growing church. And grow the church did—so much so that one year on, in September 2013, the size of the morning congregation forced a decision to run two morning services; one at 9.30, followed by a second one at 11.30.

In fact these were not the only new services that the church had introduced in 2013. In the spring of that year, following the tradition of their parent church, Holy Trinity Brompton, St Peter's opened up its first church plant. An increasing proportion of the people of the city are students, and a work had steadily developed among them, led by Alex Wood, who had joined the full-time staff team at St Peter's. He was ordained on St Peter's Day 2013, and became the Anglican Chaplain at Sussex University. He holds services at eleven o'clock on Sunday mornings at the Meeting House in the middle of university campus.

Later that year another opportunity arose to send a team, led by Richard and Catherine Merrick to the estate of Whitehawk, in the east of the city. This venture provided a means of serving some of the neediest people of the city from a base at the Anglican Church of St Cuthmans, There on 28th October, the Bishop of Chichester[6] licensed Archie Coates as Priest-in-Charge of this parish in Whitehawk and services were started on 3rd November, along with other activities on weekdays. Plans were being finalised shortly after this for another church planting venture at Hastings, which was due to be launched in autumn 2014.

At the beginning of the century there had been concerns not only about the building, but also about whether St Peter's was connecting with the vibrancy and dynamism of the city. Now, as Douglas McKittrick, who assisted the bishop at the service in Whitehawk, testifies, "St Peter's is once again, functioning as a vibrant church at the centre of a vibrant city," adding that it is, "an absolute blessing to the city of Brighton and the diocese of Chichester.... serving the new city in a new way"

This vibrancy is readily illustrated by the former Delirious? frontman, Martin Smith, who is one of many who joined St Peter's in the years immediately after the reopening. As the congregation worshipped on Easter Sunday 2013 in Sir Charles Barry's original setting, Martin led the singing of his recent composition, "God's Great Dance Floor[7]." It was a memorable occasion, with chairs being pushed to the side as worshippers filled the "open meeting-room." After all that had happened at St Peter's in recent times—and further back—the church could now sing (and say), "Let the future begin."

Notes

Chapter One: Beginnings

1. Anthony Seldon is currently the 13th Master of Wellington College, having previously been Headmaster of Brighton College
2. Seldon, A., 2002, *Brave New City*, Pomegranate Press, page 66
3. Dale, A., 1989, *Brighton Churches*, page 31
4. Grateful thanks to the East Sussex Record Office for a view of the conveyancing document, PAR/277/4/1/1
5. Brighton Gazette, 27th June 1874
6. Grateful thanks to the Brighton Museum History Room for a view of the order of service at the laying of the foundation stone
7. The Brighton Herald, 28th June 1828
8. Brighton Gazette, 27th June 1874
9. Dale, A., 1989, *Brighton Churches*, page 33
10. Dale, A., 1989, *Brighton Churches*, page 35
11. From the Brighton Churches resource in the Brighton Museum History Room
12. The Isle of Purbeck in Dorset is not far from the Isle of Portland and this contributor may well have confused Purbeck Stone with Portland Stone.
13. Burton M. and Sitwell O., 1935, *Brighton*
14. Cocke, T., *Brighton Churches—the need for action now*

Chapter Two: The Building of Brighton Churches

1. Brighton Gazette, 2nd July 1874
2. Wagner, A. and Dale, A., 1983, The Wagners of Brighton, page 28
3. Sussex Archaeological Collections, 2010: "The construction of St Peter's" by Sue Berry
4. Wagner, A. and Dale, A., 1983, *The Wagners of Brighton*, page 50
5. Carder, T. 1988, *Encyclopaedia of Brighton*
6. www.saintpaulschurch.org.uk
7. Elleray, D.R., 1981, *The Victorian Churches of Sussex*, Phillimore
8. Dale, A., 1989, *Brighton Churches*, page 36
9. Brighton Gazette, 19th December 1874

Chapter Three: The Reorganisation of Brighton Churches

1. Brighton Gazette, 2nd July 1874
2. Brighton Argus, 2nd June 1888
3. www.saintpaulschurch.org.uk
4. The Brighton Herald, 25th May 1874
5. Brighton Gazette, 23rd May 1874
6. Carder, T. 1988, *Encyclopaedia of Brighton*, page 324
7. Brighton Gazette, 2nd July 1888
8. Brighton Argus, 2nd June 1888

Chapter Four: The Addition of the Chancel

1. From the Brighton Churches resource in the Brighton Museum History Room
2. Brighton & Hove Herald, 6th June 1931
3. Dale, A., 1989, *Brighton Churches*, page 39

4. Brighton & Hove Herald, 6th June 1931
5. Brighton & Hove Herald, 6th June 1931
6. Brighton & Hove Herald, 14th September 1935
7. Sussex Daily News, 30th June 1906
8. Parish Church of St Peters—Short Guide

Chapter Five: St Peter's in the Twentieth Century

1. Carder, T. 1988, *Encyclopaedia of Brighton*, page 324
2. Brighton Argus, 3rd December 1923
3. Brighton & Hove Herald, 14th February 1942
4. St Wilfred was a seventh century Archbishop of York who is credited with the conversion of Sussex, a Kingdom in its own right and the last vestige of paganism, to Christianity
5. Brighton Argus, 11th February 1942
6. Carder, T. 1988, *Encyclopaedia of Brighton*, page 324
7. John Long was appointed organist and Master of Choristers at Beverley Cathedral in 1938.
8. Some Boyhood Memories of St Peter's by Canon Michael Long
9. Brighton & Hove Herald, 27th May 1961
10. Seldon, A., 2002, *Brave New City*, Pomegranate Press
11. Brighton Argus, 27th March 1993
12. www.mybrightonandhove.org.uk
13. East Sussex Record Office—PAR 277/7/6/4
14. Carder, T. 1988, *Encyclopaedia of Brighton*, page 324
15. Brighton Argus, 5th September 1985
16. Furlong, M., 2000, *the C of E: The State It's In*, S.P.C.K.

17. The author is most grateful to Bishop Dominic Walker for his recollections
18. St Peter's Parish Records
19. St Peter's Church Log Book, 1994-2005
20. St Peter's Quinquennial Report, 1981

Chapter Six: The Threat of Closure

1. The author is most grateful to Archdeacon McKittrick for his recollections
2. When the union of St Peter's and the Chapel Royal had taken place it had been stipulated that both churches would remain financially independent of each other.
3. The author is most grateful to Father David Biggs for his recollections
4. Brighton Argus, 24th June 2003
5. The author is most grateful to the Revd Peter Irwin-Clark for his recollections
6. Brighton Argus, 5th April 2005
7. Brighton and Hove Leader, 7th June 2007
8. Brighton Argus, 19th September 2007
9. Brighton Argus, 7th October 2007
10. Brighton Argus, 9th September 2006

Chapter Seven: Holy Trinity Brompton

1. The author is most grateful to the Revd Archie Coates for his recollections
2. The author is most grateful to Mrs Jean Calder for her recollections
3. Friends of St Peter's Church, Annual Report 2008

4. Letter from Canon Michael Long to Jean Calder, 23rd May 2008
5. Brighton Argus, 8th May 2008
6. Brighton Argus, 30th October 2009
7. Brighton Argus, 31st October 2009

Chapter Eight: Serving the People of the City

1. The author is most grateful to the Revd Jonny Gumbel for his recollections
2. Carder, T. 1988, Encyclopaedia of Brighton, page 324
3. Simon Dyson, HMDW Architects Ltd, December 2012
4. The author is most grateful to Mrs Becky Atkins, the Operations Coordinator at St Peter's Brighton for her help in providing data
5. Brighton Argus, 12th October 2012
6. Martin Warner had succeeded John Hind as Bishop of Chichester on 3rd May 2012. He was pictured on the day of his appointment being greeted by Archie and Sam Coates outside St Peter's
7. The words of the chorus of "God's Great Dance Floor" are:
    "You'll never stop loving us
    No matter how far we run
    You'll never give up on us
    All of heaven shouts
    Let the future begin"

Index

Appendix: List of Incumbents of St Peters

Thomas Cooke (Perpetual Curate, 1828-1873)
John Hannah (Vicar, 1873-1887)
John Julius Hannah (Vicar, 1888-1902)
Benedict Hoskyns (Vicar, 1902-1917)
Francis Dormer Pierce (Vicar, 1917-1923)
Frederick Hicks (Vicar, 1924-1927)
Alfred Rose (Vicar, 1928-1935)
John How (Vicar, 1935-1938)
Geoffrey Warde (Vicar, 1939-1944)
Norman Robathan (Vicar, 1945-1953)
David Booth (Vicar, 1953-1959)
John Keeling (Vicar, 1960-1974)
John Hester (Vicar, 1975-1985)
Dominic Walker (Vicar, 1985-1997)
Douglas McKittrick (Vicar, 1997-2002)
David Biggs (Priest-in-charge 2002-2009)
Archie Coates (Vicar, 2009—)